AROUND THE
CHANNEL
ISLANDS

CATHERINE ROTHWELL

The
History
Press

First published 2008

Reprinted in 2014 by
The History Press
The Mill, Brimscombe Port,
Stroud, Gloucestershire, GL5 2QG
www.thehistorypress.co.uk

Copyright © Catherine Rothwell, 2008

Title page photograph: Rozel, 1930s.

British Library Cataloguing in Publication Data
A catalogue record for this book is available from
the British Library.

ISBN 978-0-7509-4958-3

Typeset in 11/13.5 Sabon.
Printed and bound in Great Britain by
Marston Book Services Limited, Oxfordshire

To the late John Charles Houghton,
who knew and loved the Channel Islands.

St Peter Port from the harbour, Guernsey.

CONTENTS

Vegetable Market, St Helier, Jersey.

AUTHOR'S NOTE

Some years ago, in a popular TV series, actor John Nettles as Sergeant Bergerac brought additional fame to Jersey and fostered interest in the Channel Islands' tourist industry. Indeed, he came to personify the lovely island of Jersey so I was indeed delighted during the preparation of this book to

receive an encouraging message from John as follows: 'Herewith photograph and this as permission to use it in your book. Best of luck with it!' He signed it! I was thrilled and I still treasure it, echoing as it does the kindness my late husband and I met with during our time in Jersey.

The message on one of my old postcards reads 'We are having a fine time in Jersey and have no wish to return home.' Praise indeed.

We ourselves rejoiced in all weathers in many counties, but of Jersey, ther overriding memory was of sunshine and the good effect it always had on people's spirits, whether islander or holiday-maker.

As John Nettles said in those days, 'It's all here, just waiting to be discovered.' My hope is that the magic of this discovery will be enhanced by these old photographs and facts from days gone by.

Catherine Rothwell

INTRODUCTION

As a collector of islands, I have written local history books on Man and Wight, visited Corfu, Gozo, Paxos, Crete, Cyprus, Santorini, Sicily and Rhodes, so it seemed reasonable in retrospect to assemble a number of old photographs and picture postcards found over the years in Jersey, Guernsey, Sark, Herm and Alderney.

Photography is in my blood, although full interest did not blossom until I was fifty, for not until then did I start to collect old photographs. My father, who was born in the 1870s, always referred to himself as a 'pioneer photographer'. I recall him also as an inventor and dilettante, dabbling in anything new, ventures which often brought discomfort to the family in their train, but occasionally shining success. Life was never dull! Father reminded me of a certain Rufus Porter; their lives never touched but overlapped by ten years. Rufus was sign-writer, editor, portrait painter and musician, who invented a Camera Obscura and a revolving almanac besides a flying ship, a corn sheller, a churn and a washing machine. My father invented a reflex camera under the short-lived Paxman Camera Company banner, developed from the Houghton

The author receiving an award at the Lakeland Book of the Year, 2006.

Folding Reflex Camera, ligher than the heavy plate with which he got such good results and for which he made a special carrying-box covered with fine leather. Having purchased an improved mineral oil Russian Iron Lantern for £4 10s, fitted with a 3-inch wick paraffin lamp and brass stage, he was not satisfied and designed his own magic lantern, which at first try-out set the kitchen table on fire. With his own camera, chemicals and portable dark room he visited Wales, Dublin, Anglesey, Yorkshire, Lancashire and Devon, but few of Clement Houghton's photographs survive although there were stacks of glass negatives kept in a zinc bath. His Briggs cousins shared the interest and when the R101 airship went over their house Father climbed through the glass fanlight onto the roof, presumably to get a shot of the dirigible as he called it. He, who loved long words, applied them fittingly. In spite of lameness inflicted by what was then called infantile paralysis, he was amazingly agile; in youth the champion one-legged skater of his district. To the consternation of visiting air-raid wardens in the early days of the Second World War, he leapt onto the table to repair the sagging blackout, promptly driving a nail through the gas pipe, a deficiency not discovered till the next day. Poor mother! These 'misloriments' were legion, but both my brother and I in later years gratefully developed interest in father's profession, Edward photographing nature and I for ever searching out those old views of people, ships, streets, fashions, shops, trains and trams which tell such a remarkable story of times past.

The dramatic beauty, interest and quality of light in Jersey, Alderney, Herm and Sark thrilled him and especially the Guernsey cattle for he loved animals; we never had fewer than three cats. What Emerson called 'the sure chemistry of time' has transmuted the early photographer's day represented in this island collection with a kindly ambient light. I hope it gives as much pleasure to the reader as I have had in its loving yet poignant assemblage of 'the magic isles'.

Catherine Rothwell, 2008

PART ONE

Jersey

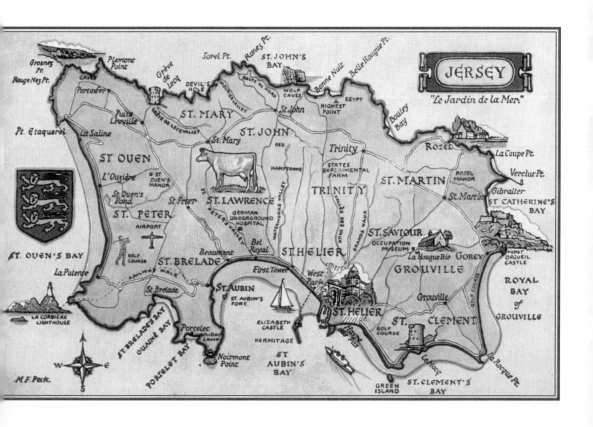

A composite postcard showing views of Jersey, 1933.

Typical of thousands of postcards sent to France and Britain in the 1930s the scenes depicted on this 1933 postcard together with others are enlarged upon in these pages. Being in an enviable geographical position in the Gulf of St Malo, the Channel Islands are part of the British Isles, not a colony or a dominion, but with much independence. Two Bailiwicks, of which Jersey is one, each have a Lieutenant Governor or Bailiff. Jersey has its own separate House of Parliament called the States. Before the Norman Conquest the Channel Islands were part of the Dukedom of Normandy, governed by representatives of the Duke even after William the Conqueror became King of England. When England lost her French possessions in King John's reign, the Channel Islands remained to her, thus they are possessions of the rulers of England but distinct from the latter's control, which lies with Privy Council advised by the Home Secretary. The Bailiffs, always Channel Islanders, displaced the King's Warden but archaic laws and customs, notably Clameur de Haro, the ancient right of the islander to call for justice for his person and property, have been retained.

Len and Hetty, who sent this postcard to Leeds, had visited all the places on this composite postcard and were 'having lovely weather, the sun shining all day long' in 1933.

Halkett Place, St Helier, *c.* 1890.

This view of Halkett Place, St Helier, dates from over a century ago. On the left is the chemist's shop of F.G. Piquet, with a lady approaching in skirts sweeping down to the ground; a youth with a handcart crosses the road and in the distance are other wheeled, horse-drawn vehicles. At the turn of the nineteenth century St Helier consisted of a narrow strip of cottages stretching from Snow Hill to Charing Cross, and with the Governor living at Gorey, there was no indication that it would become the most important town on Jersey. Less than 170 years ago there were hardly any roads and people travelled everywhere on horseback or in horse-drawn carts. However, as time went on, the St Helier Market attracted people from all over the island, the town grew rapidly in size and by 1969 the population had risen to 26,484.

Halkett Place, St Helier, *c.* 1910.

This scene is further down Halkett Place some twenty years later than the photograph on page 9, with increased horse-drawn traffic in evidence. On the right alongside the famous market is a shop selling Jaeger clothing, hallmark in those days of excellence in pure woollen underwear, known to be purchased by bishops and George Bernard Shaw. Halkett Place held markets for cattle, fish and vegetables, but the new Market Buildings covering about 10,000 square yards took the premier position. In the centre an ornamental fountain played above a fernery and fish pond. In the 1920s and '30s it was reported that markets held on Wednesdays and Saturdays were most interesting. Not only could visitors delight in an excellent supply of fruit, vegetables and flowers; they could also hear an interesting babble of English, French and Anglo-Norman. Halkett Place led northward out of King and Queen Streets to the Central Post Office and Telegraph Offices of the town.

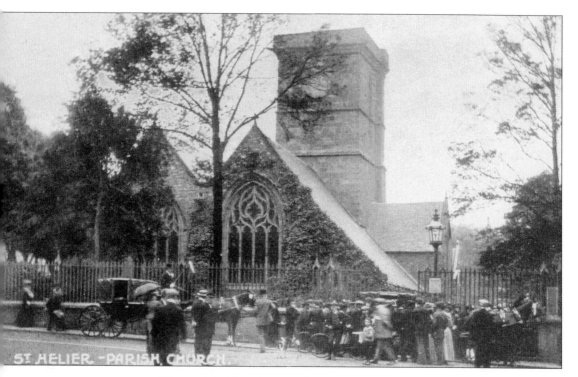

The Parish Church, St Helier, early 1900s.

The horse-drawn landau with groom bears witness to the early 1900s date of this excellent photograph of the Parish Church of St Helier. Judging by the crowds and carriages, the occasion may well be an important wedding.

One of the twelve parish churches of the island, the foundation dates from the middle of the fourteenth century. It was restored between 1863 and 1867, retaining its square tower under which was buried the body of brave Major Pierson who perished at the Battle of Jersey. The Norrey family vault is also found here. Their arms can be seen on one of the gateways of Mont Orgueil Castle, and Maximilian Norrey served in the army of Henry IV, King of France and Navarre. During the Hundred Years War with France the church bell would ring to warn of attack and citizens barricaded themselves inside; it was also a refuge where criminals were safe from arrest. The organ, which was placed in the church in 1922, was considered to be the finest in the Channel Islands.

Beresford Street, early 1900s.

On the northern side of the market building was Beresford Street across from which was the vegetable market and the fish market. Abundant displays of fruit, vegetables, flowers and fish, especially at the time of this photograph, demonstrated the benefits of the Jersey climate.

Along with Halkett Place, Beresford Street was known to have the best shops. Visitors in the 1920s and '30s were advised on wet days 'to visit the markets and Beresford Street.'

A traditional harvest was the supply of vraic or seaweed which was burnt in the hearth for cooking and heating, the ash making excellent fertiliser. Dates were laid down as to when seaweed could be collected and trips to the beach in farm carts on March days were eagerly anticipated; cider, large buns and raw limpets being consumed by the harvesters. In later years the gathering of seaweed was strictly controlled.

The Promenade, St Helier, 1904.

In this 1904 photograph we see the Promenade with Olympia Winter Gardens on the far right. St Helier was the catchment area for most of the Channel Islands' 60,000 visitors. Before the First World War and the fall of the franc Jersey received a large number of visitors from France.

Its extensive promenade close to the island's valley scenery and beautiful woods accounted for most of its popularity, but by the 1920s it was also the starting point of two railways and the centre of bus and car services.

Facing the sea and harbour and most centrally situated for railway stations, the oldest established hotel on the island was by 1920 called the Royal Yacht Hotel, and had excursion cars, starting from its door twice daily during the season.

St Helier Harbour, 1895.

St Helier Harbour, 1950.

More views of St Helier showing the extensive harbour in the days when sailing ships still plied the seven seas. From the landing stage on the pier the visitor passed between the Western Railway station and the Weighbridge Gardens where a statue of Queen Victoria was erected in 1890. From Albert Pier in the 1920s was a daily service, Sundays excepted, via Guernsey to Southampton and from North Quay at 7.45 a.m. to Weymouth. These services ran from mid-July to the end of September. Signals on a flagpole, explained by the local Royal Almanac, indicated the arrival or departure of mail boats, steamers and other vessels and also warned of approaching storms. It is interesting to learn that when a vessel was in sight of Corbière Lighthouse, flags indicating the company owning it were run up the flagpole. The oldest part of the harbour is the Old South Pier, which was begun in 1700.

The Weighbridge and Old Harbour, *c.* 1900.

This photograph of the Weighbridge and Old Harbour in about 1900 is full of interest and movement. Dozens of horses pulling loaded carts are lining up in readiness for barrels and containers to be loaded onto waiting ships. On the right are warehouses with more wagons and horses in the distance. For safe loading on a terribly dangerous coast, good harbourage was of the utmost importance and the States spent huge sums of money to achieve this. Berths for mail steamers were specially dredged but arrival and departure of other vessels depended on the tides. Six miles of quays were available in this large harbour, but in 1923 a further scheme at a cost of £200,000 was mooted to enlarge the harbour and meet the requirements of new steamers being built by the railway companies.

The Weighbridge and West Park, 1953.

Another view of the Weighbridge and West Park, St Helier, but some sixty years later than the one on page 15. To the left is the splendid Esplanade and some of St Helier's many hotels. On the far right in the foreground the Southampton Family and Residential Hotel can be seen across from Weighbridge Gardens facing the Harbour Approach. The statue of Queen Victoria, already alluded to, can be seen in the midst of its flowerbeds and grass plots. Some horse and cart traffic is still in use but a single-deck bus and motorcar show that the era of the combustion engine has arrived. From this point Mulcaster Street leading to the Parish Church, Conway Street, Bond Street and Broad Street leading to the General Post Office were all handy for arriving visitors. In Bond Street they could seek out the Southern Railway and the Great Western Railway offices.

The home of Victor Hugo.

The ornate surroundings beloved by Victor Hugo who lived in both Jersey and Guernsey are shown in this early twentieth-century postcard. On the left is a valuable, silk-covered Pluvinet chair; the statues are Italian.

Victor Hugo, exiled from France in 1851, lived for a time at 3 Marina Terrace, Havre de Pas, now the Maison Victor Hugo Hotel. Other exiled Frenchmen ran a political magazine jointly with Hugo, *L'Homme*. It was not long before they were all asked to leave Jersey, whereupon Guernsey became their next choice. The publication contained Hugo's spirited criticism of Queen Victoria for her French Government leanings and was severely frowned upon by the patriotic islanders. In his childhood, Lawrence of Arabia was a visitor to Havre de Pas where race meetings were once held on the sands.

The Esplanade, 1904.

This photograph of The Esplanade showing the Bristol Hotel on the left, canopied deckchairs, umbrellas held against the sun, and graceful Edwardian clothing worn by the ladies, one seen pushing a bassinette with huge wheels, dates from 1904. The French had discovered 'Jersey Esplanade' but there were not yet many English. Perhaps seasickness was feared, although a remedy – Mothersill's seasick remedy – was available in the early 1900s. Howard's Aspirin Tablets were made by a firm already established for 100 years and travellers were advised, 'Never travel without a bottle of Dr J. Collis Browne's Chlorodyne, the best remedy known . . . acts like a charm.'

On this stretch of The Esplanade, known as First Tower, there was good bathing accommodation provided by machines and also a Men's Bathing Place near the stunted tower called La Collette. This area, which at high water was surrounded by the sea, held 150 'dressing boxes'.

The Bathing Pool, or La Piscine, early 1930s.

The Bathing Pool, with Ladies' Cabins on the right, was always popular and Jersey was blessed with the right weather for an open-air pool. In 1926 it was stated, 'The climate of the Channel Islands is the most perfect Great Britain can boast.'

Two extensive pools of sea water, one known as Victoria Marine Lake, controlled by the West End Bathing Company, the other at Havre de Pas, were retained by circular walls. Mixed bathing was permissible at all times, a single ticket at the Victoria Marine Lake costing sixpence in 1927.

The 5-acre sea-water surface of West End Bathing Pool was covered at every tide; thus the water was renewed twice a day. Rafts, springboards and a double diving stage, with a boatman always in attendance, made this one of the most popular venues in St Helier.

The Pavilion, 1935.

'Having plenty of sun and sea bathing, weather continues fine and warm,' read the words on the back of this postcard sent in July 1935. West Park Pavilion, shown here, was close to West Park station and the Victoria Marine Lake already referred to. The Pavilion had beautiful rock gardens aflame with cushions of saxifrage, aubretia and rock cress in early spring. An added bonus towards the end of of the year was 'a long sunny autumn called St Martin's Summer which begins about 10 October.'

On Sundays and some weekdays bands played in Triangle Park or in the Pavilion if wet. Also in West Park concert troupes appeared. By 1926 the 'talking pictures' had arrived. West's Picture Palace in Peter Street, the Alhambra in Phillips Street, the Picture House in Don Street and Opera House in Gloucester Street all gave regular shows. More concerts, shows and sports were available at Springfield Grounds and Pavilion off St Mark's Road.

The Market, early 1900s.

This detailed photograph of the market which dates from the early 1900s includes a boy with handcart, probably accompanying the photographer. The old sett roadways, strong-built hall with its arches and elegant hanging lamps, are shown to perfection in empty streets. The early photographer always excited interest and a small group have posed behind the boy to watch proceedings. The large site of the new Market Buildings which was to bring much prosperity to St Helier was then a novelty. Beresford Street ran along the northern side and Hill Street, La Motte Street, Le Coie and St Saviour's Road, all parts of an important thoroughfare near the Court House, were close to this important nucleus, known to all as 'The Markets'.

The Parade and Cenotaph, 1930.

This picture of the Parade and Centoaph was published in about 1930. Skirts are shorter and a few motorcars are in evidence: heavy, high vehicles with running boards and splendid, large headlamps. The Royal Parade with lawns and avenues of trees has the fine statue of General Don discernable to the right of the Cenotaph. General Don, as Lieutenant Governor during the Napoleonic period, worked indefatigably for the island of Jersey. He made excellent roads and erected batteries for coastal defence. A well-trained militia was also a feature of his ministry.

The Cenotaph commemorates the men of Jersey who fell in two world wars. At the meeting point of the walks is a granite pedestal supporting a bronze bust of a Mayor of St Helier, P. Baudains, who held office for fifteen years.

St Ouen's Manor.

About a mile from St Peter's is a stately mansion reminiscent of a French chateau, photographed here perhaps ninety years ago. The building originally formed a twelfth-century castle, which was enlarged in the seventeenth century. In 1890 complete restoration resulted in the addition of the two towers behind the south wing. St Ouen's Manor was for thirty-two generations the home of the De Carteret family. Sir Philip De Carteret is commemorated on a brass plate in the church of the village of St Ouen. His family shaped much of Jersey's history.

The bay of St Ouen's is on the west side of Jersey, the largest inlet in the Channel Islands, not popular in early years as visitors thought it bleak and bare. The full force of a south-westerly gale at St Ouen's in winter is in stark contrast to the almost sub-tropical aspects presented in other parts of the island. In 1651 Parliamentary forces brought by Admiral Blake's fleet landed in this sweeping bay, a main source of vraic, and overcame the Royalists.

St Peter's Valley, 1901.

The building on the left in this 1901 photograph of St Peter's Valley is the Victoria Hotel. Also at St Peter's was the Alexandra in the days when boarding cost no more than 3 guineas a week. The average charge was 6*s* to 10*s* a day for a double room. This beautiful valley was one of the favourite places for wagonette rides. Drawn by four horses controlled by a top-hatted groom who knew the countryside well, on fine days these rides would work up an appetite. The Victoria was a calling place for food and refreshment; fresh local lobster and cream teas being the favourite fare. Visitors could see at the junction of St Peter's Roads an old gun with an interesting inscription: 'Joh Owyn made thys pese anno domini 1551 for the paryshe of Saynt Peter in Jersse.'

'The views in all directions are fine,' it was reported in 1920, with the wooded valley, dark trees and brilliant blue waters of St Aubin's Bay seen from the heights. Behind the Victoria Hotel are well-tended St Peter's Vineries on whose sun-drenched slopes grapes have been cultivated since Roman times.

Vinchelez Lane, 1903.

E.H. Toovey's charming photograph of young girls in Vinchelez Lane was taken in 1903. The old stone gateway leads into the grounds of the Manor House. This lane, its trees meeting overhead as in a Cornish lane, with sunlight filtering through, is reminiscent in spring of a cathedral and is in the vicinity of Plémont with its Needle Rock and Douet de la Mer where visitors could see a waterfall. Motor vehicles running to the Plémont Hotel offered 'something new in Motor Coaching': Jackie Boy or the Silent Guide, 'a novel invention coupled with specially prepared itineraries for imparting and retaining information in a pleasing manner about places of interest you may visit or pass en route on favourite motor coach tours.'

In those wonderful days it was possible to buy a man's Aquascutum full-length, pure wool, weatherproof coat for 6 guineas.

Rozel Lane, 1923.

A lake on the right of this photograph from 1923 was a particularly noted beauty spot. The entrance to Rozel Manor, situated in a well-timbered park, may be where the solitary figure in the donkey cart is heading. If special permission was obtained, a chapel with Norman architecture in the grounds could be viewed. Rozel Bay itself is on a fine stretch of coast noted for its fishing. In the 1930s catches of lobster, shrimps, bass, bream, conger eel, mullet and whiting were reported off Les Ecrehous, a group of rocky islets. An old man known as King Pinel lived on the largest of these, Maître Ile, where the ruins of a monastery built in 1203 by monks from Normandy were situated, both being tourists attractions. A short pier then sheltered the fishing boats of this area, whose ancient name meant a place of reeds. Sandier than Bouley Bay, Rozel Bay was always popular with boat owners.

In the Swiss Valley, 1909.

During the summer in 1925 motor coaches left the open space at the Weighbridge, St Helier, daily at 11 a.m. and 2.30 p.m. for various parts of the island, the general charge for a full day trip was 4s; there were also evening trips. Picturesque places like the Swiss Valley, seen here in 1909, were voted 'lovely, our diggings A.1.' A sample route was St Brelade's Bay, St Peter's Church, St Aubin coast road and St Helier. St Aubin was Jersey's original port with a small harbour built in 1675. By 1926 St Brelade's Bay had Kalima Hall with its maple-floored ballroom, an ideal summer and winter residence standing in its own grounds.

During the sixteenth and seventeenth centuries when tourism was virtually unknown, the famous pullover or Jersey which took its name from the island, along with the knitted stockings provided the main industry. Even the men knitted these popular garments, later sold to visitors and sent abroad. The States had to pass a law forbidding men to knit from March to November as it was affecting the cutting of seaweed and the gathering in of the harvest.

St Brelade's Church, 1930s.

Five and a half miles from St Helier and one and a half from St Aubin is St Brelade's Church, shown in this postcard from the 1930s. Adjoining the church is the Fisherman's Chapel, 43ft long and 18ft wide, which dates back to the sixth century – the oldest place of worship on the island. The walls, in which there are five small windows, are 3ft thick and the roof made of small stones. Frescoes on the ceiling were discovered by accident when rain leaking through the roof saturated the plaster and threw colours into high relief, the most famous being The Annunciation, dating from between 1320 and 1330. The Germans used the graveyard of St Brelade's as the military cemetery during the Occupation, and 213 soldiers were buried there. An early visitor to St Brelade's Bay was John Keble who, in the eighteenth century, wanted to keep it a secret, fearing it would be spoiled. However, long before that the original inhabitants of Jersey must have lived there for evidence of early man, flint instruments and teeth have been found at La Cotte Point.

'Adventures of a Runaway'.

These steps were the scene of a horse's sensational feat, a depiction of which found its way onto thousands of postcards for visitors to send home. The horse bolted down these sixty-six steps, dragging a cart, to run on a mile before it was finally stopped. This particular card was posted on 14 July 1905 with a note to Mrs Copley, 'Just one more for your collection.'

The Common at Crouville, not far from this scene, was also historic in that duels were fought there. A carnival used to be held there annually, too. The Queen's Valley adjoining the Common has the remains of the oldest windmill on the island, dating from 1331, used today as a landmark for ships. A certain type of fig introduced from South Africa, the Hottentot fig, with yellow-red flowers, bloomed here and botanists sought the Jersey fern, the only annual fern in Britain, seen nowhere else except in Jersey and Guernsey.

The Battle of Jersey, 1781.

A replica of the Battle of Jersey hangs in the Court House, Royal Square. This was fought close to the Peirson Hotel, which had bullet marks to prove it, but during renovation lost them so imitation bullet marks were painted in. On 1 January 1781 a French soldier of fortune, with the approval of the French King, sailed with 1,200 men and after shooting the guard and taking prisoner the Lieutenant General, Major Moses Corbet, occupied Royal Square and demanded surrender. In charge at St Ouen, twenty-four-year-old Major Peirson of the 95th Regiment, the Sherwood Foresters, hastily collected companies of the Jersey Militia and set off for Royal Square where, despite calls to surrender, he entered by the narrow street later called Peirson Place and closed with the enemy in hand-to-hand combat. Peirson was killed but his men battled on, urged by Philip Dumaresq, a subaltern who assumed command and turned defeat into victory. Rullecour, the soldier who had instigated the siege, was killed with twenty-six Frenchmen, while another 100 lay severely wounded; 500 prisoners were taken and the remainder fled. Two hundred years later J. Rowland of 15 The Esplanade issued this postcard picture.

The Battle of Flowers, 1904.

Albert Smith, professional photographer, offered to attend at the shortest notice. He developed and printed snapshots in twenty-four hours and had dark rooms available for amateurs. This is one of his photographs, taken on 18 August 1904, showing Jersey's annual event, the Battle of Flowers. At this stage of the parade the fire brigade with decorated horses has arrived on what is obviously a beautiful day. Taking place in Victoria Avenue, it involved a procession of all sorts of vehicles from cycles, hand carts, lorries, landaus, to double-decker buses adorned with flowers, from the days when the floats were pulled apart at the end of the parade and people pelted with flowers. The Battle of Flowers Association awards prizes at the end of the procession and nowadays petals are dropped on the crowds from a helicopter.

Charlie Chaplin, as a member of Fred Karno's concert party, took part in one battle which, it is said, led to his first film part and eventual worldwide fame.

Grève de Lecq, 1940s.

This bay photographed in the 1940s, between Plémont Point and Sorel Point, home of 'Old Nick' (see below), is small but lovely with a firm, sandy beach. From the Mourier waterfall which cascades down the smooth cliff face, a narrow path skirts the cliff into the Devil's Hole, but only the young and sure-footed were advised to attempt it. Legend has it that approaching stormy nights at Grève de Lecq are heralded by the cry of the sea, for when the forty families left Jersey in 1565 to colonise Sark, one ship carrying children struck the reefs. Sailors ever since have said a paternoster (hence Paternoster Rocks) because the ghostly cries of the doomed children are said to warn of storms.

The Devil's Hole, 1900s.

This fantastic replica of the Devil was met by visitors to Creux de Vis in the 1900s. The figure with horns and tail was once kept in a cage and when a rope was pulled from inside, it nodded its head. The hole or creux, a crater 200ft deep and 100ft across to which the wooden staircase gave access, has a long, dark tunnel leading out to sea. The view of the tide rushing through this tunnelled entrance and over great boulders remains quite spectacular to visitors. During the winding walk in the 1960s, a bronze-coloured fibreglass Devil, placed in the middle of a pond for safe keeping, was suddenly encountered. Further down was where the devil in this photograph stood, but history records that three models have been stolen.

Bonne Nuit Bay, 1923.

Bonne Nuit Bay presents a peaceful picture in July 1923. A famous spot from Fremont Point, the western horn of Bonne Nuit Bay, was the Wolf's Cave at the foot of a narrow cleft running inland, at that time labelled 'the most picturesque and romantic cave in Jersey.'

Admission was 3*d*, and was obtained through a refreshment pavilion. Steep, zig-zag paths to the foot of the chine were trodden when the tide was low to meet the proprietor, torch in hand, ready to conduct groups down an iron ladder leading to the floor of the cave. At low tide, groups could pass via the sandy floor of the cave to the Venus Bath, a very clear rock pool, but when the tide was up, one could only stand on the ladder and watch its surge. Sheer, heather-covered cliffs surround Bonne Nuit Bay where in the middle is a rock known as Le Cheval Guillaume, now called Cheval Rock, connected with an ancient ritual. People from all over the island would gather on Midsummer Day to row round the rock, thus avoiding bad luck for a whole year, and the fishermen took part too, to ensure a good harvest from the sea.

St Aubin's Bay.

By a seafront road, with so many other delightful bays close by and quick access to beautiful scenery inland, St Aubin was always popular. Leading up through the village was a valley road beside the railway among wooded hills dotted with 'cottages smothered in roses, honeysuckle and greenery'. In the seventeenth century the tidal harbour was full of vessels captured by Sir George Carteret, privateer and Governor of the island. Charles I made Sir George a Vice Admiral to lend respectability to his ways but British merchants lost so much that Cromwell sent Admiral Blake to take possession of Jersey. In this bay, wooded down to the sea's edge, St Aubin's Fort was built in Henry VIII's reign to protect the town – as St Aubin was once the capital.

Jesse Boot, founder of the famous chain of chemists' shops, is linked with St Aubin through the 'Glass Church'. Commissioned by his wife in 1934, St Matthew's, with its Lalique glass altar, glass cross and unique glass front is virtually a memorial to Jesse Boot, Lord Trent.

St Ouen's Bay, 1936.

St Ouen's Bay in 1936 displays a desolate and lonely aspect. During the Occupation strong fortifications appeared and buildings were razed. A German gun bunker, one of the remnants, is to be found in the grounds of Etacquerel Guest House. By the 1960s when it cost only 1s an hour to hire a surfboard, the bay was discovered, the sport being introduced from America. A competition is organised every June which attracts entrants from France, Australia, the USA and Britain, the bay being renowned for its enormous breakers. Here the Jersey Surf Club set up its headquarters. A 200ft-high rock called the Pinnacle, once a place of worship, rises sheer at the north-west corner of the bay.

Near the artificial pond at St Ouen's Bay is des Monts Grantez dolmen, opened in 1912. This ancient burial place revealed a skeleton leaning against the passage wall. More bodies were found in the tomb beyond, together with colourful stones and shells.

Two views of Portelet Bay and Janvrin Island.

The island in the middle of Portelet Bay, approached at high water, is where the entire crew of a vessel died of plague while their ship was in quarantine. The last to die was the captain, Phillipe Janvrin, whose name the island has borne ever since. Phillipe, who was buried on the island on 27 September 1721, was in sight of his home but dared not land. The registers at St Brelade's contain a record of his burial as the service was held there, but the coffin was not allowed. Between Noirmont Point on the east and Fret Point on the west is Portelet Bay with chapel and village on the table land high above. A Martello tower called Janvrin's Tower, part of the defences against invasion from France, can be seen on top of the island, but this was not actually built until 1811.

Gorey and Mont Orgueil Castle.

Gorey and Mont Orgueil Castle – the great feature of eastern Jersey. The Jersey Eastern Railway took visitors from St Helier to Gorey in 25 minutes, the terminus being Gorey Pier from where a steep road and 244 steps led up to the castle, whose visitors' book has an entry: 'Her Majesty the Queen visited this Castle September 3rd. 1846.' It stands proudly on the headland of porphyric rock, separating Grouville Bay from St Catherine's Bay, its highest part being 310ft above the sea. Before the introduction of cannon, Mont Orgueil was impregnable. The English were said to be so jealous for this castle, that no Frenchman was allowed to enter unless blindfolded. The castle resisted two important French attacks, one in the Hundred Years War from Philip de Valois and another from Bertrand du Guesclin, Constable of France, who managed to make his mark but as the English fleet hove to, had to retreat. The Puritan, William Prynne, was imprisoned here for his attack on the theatre, maypoles, music, hunting and false hair, things he deemed appertaining to the Devil. It was the Duke of Clarence in Henry V's reign who first called it Mont Orgueil, which was a common name for a strong fort. From the top of the castle on a clear day the coast of France can be seen and in very favourable conditions, Mont St Michel.

Gorey became famous in the early nineteenth century for its rich oyster beds which the islanders had to themselves until they were dredged by fishing fleets from England, rendering them barren by 1864. While the oysters flourished, a small pier was built, now used for pleasure boats.

The rocks and Corbière Lighthouse.

The Corbière Lighthouse was built in 1874 on a rock rising 90ft above high water. The light itself, 135ft above sea level, can be seen over a distance of 17 miles, showing alternately white and red. Mariners were further warned in foggy weather by an alarm bell and automatic firing of explosives. Many vessels have been lost over hundreds of years at this treacherous point. At low tide a causeway links the point with the lighthouse and visitors enjoyed toiling up the ninety-five steps, although they were not allowed to enter. In the 1920s the railway terminus was near the point. Visitors called at Corbière Tea Room, then went on to the cove of La Rosière, the pirates' caves and the smugglers' caves by following a concrete path made over the rocks. In 1946 assistant lighthouse keeper Peter Larbelestier was drowned trying to rescue a visitor cut off by the tide. A siren is now sounded when the causeway is about to be covered.

At Corbière Point was a large house, the residence of the lighthouse keepers. Reddish granite composes most of the jagged rocks and there existed a quarry which worked the rose-red stone. One huge rock known as Table des Marthes was probably once part of a prehistoric tomb. North from the lighthouse a road led to St Aubin's Bay. Tourists could take a short cut at Petit Port Bay, crossing a low, sandy hill to the main road. To visit the lighthouse in the 1890s a permit had to be sought from the Secretariat at the Hôtel de Ville. Corbière, designed by Imrie Bell, was the first lighthouse in Great Britain to be built of concrete. The rocky promontory of La Corbière is full of caves used by smugglers in the nineteenth century. One cave with a massive pillar in the centre, a great tourist draw, was probably used by early man.

Postcard views of Plémont.

'How we were rescued at Plémont' features in many postcards dating from around 1910. It was customary to carry the ladies through a pool in the most westerly cave. 'There is nothing remarkable to see when the trip has been made but it is fairly popular,' said the guide books of the day. Motor vehicles ran up to Plémont Hotel where a hut to the right of the hotel was of special interest as it featured in Sir Gilbert Parker's story about Jersey, 'The Battle of the Strong'. From here, Guernsey, Herm and Jethou, with Sark 9 miles distant and Alderney on the horizon, were pointed out, also the long stretch of French coast. Not far away are the ruins of Grosnez Castle at the top of sheer cliffs 200ft above sea level, believed to have been built as a refuge after the French had massacred 1,500 islanders in one raid.

Very high cliffs and a large number of caves at Plémont were favourite places to visit. A fee of 2*d* was charged in 1926 for crossing a series of bridges. One passage under natural arches led to the Waterfall Cave shown in the 1942 photograph (above, left). A stream of water falls from the cliff, especially dramatic after a rainstorm. From this cave the cable connecting Jersey with Guernsey went out. Some of the lofty caves are almost 200ft long and one, up the cliff face and smaller, was inhabited during the Stone Age. Small implements, bones and other signs have been discovered. A spring on the headland, Fontaine Martin, was thought by some islanders to confer magical powers of sight if the eyes were bathed in its cool waters at new moon, but only if it fell on Sunday.

Druids' Monument, St Martin, 1900s.

In Jersey are a number of Druids' monuments. This dolmen, photographed in the 1900s, was at St Martin. Of prehistoric remains on the island the finest is the Hougue Bie, an ancient Neolithic burial place situated between Gorey and St Helier, a large, circular mound whose depths hide a passage grave considered by some archaeologists to be the finest in Western Europe.

Besides Druids, Jersey has a history of witches and the meeting place of the Jersey witches where they held their sabbaths was St Clement's Bay. An outcrop of rock has become known as the witches' rock, which bears two marks supposedly made by the Devil's hoof. Records of two so-called witches who were condemned to death occur in 1585 and 1648.

Milking time, 1910.

The gentle, far-famed Jersey cow features in a truly pastoral scene early in the twentieth century. The milkmaid wears a traditional sun bonnet and the long, voluminous skirt of the female farm worker. The true Jersey animal is honey or smoke-coloured, shaded on the haunches, with deer-like face and black, short horns, producing milk extremely rich in cream, and butter which knows no rival. Stringent laws on the island safeguard the breeding of these beautiful, useful animals, every farmer appreciating the necessity to preserve the strain. The Jersey cow was usually tethered by a chain in order to restrict the area grazed and to prevent over-eating; at intervals its place of herbage was moved.

In the nineteenth century food for islanders consisted of beans and potatoes, fish, conger eel soup or rabbit with Jersey Simnel cake or a most unusual apple pie for special occasions. Traditionally, cider was the drink for all islanders and every house and farm had a cider press.

Jersey's famous 10ft cabbages.

In the photograph above, which dates from the late 1920s, Jersey cows are measured against cabbages 10ft high whose fabulous size always amazed and amused visitors. The stalks, made into walking sticks, have been sold as souvenirs. These unique Jersey walking sticks could be purchased in the late 1950s from M.P. le Gresley's woodcarving centre at L'Etacq. The stalks, when dry, become amazingly hard and lend themselves to carving. The desire to possess one of these sticks was known in the 1920s as 'Jersey fever'. Clogs, figurines and bowls were also available. At the same time the Jersey Pottery at Gorey Village was run by Clive Jones and family in a beautiful rose garden setting where the entire process of pottery-making could be observed.

The type of cabbage shown in the photographs was produced for animal feed and nicknamed Long Jack, but its general cultivation died out in the early 1900s.

St Brelade's Bay, mid-1950s.

A family visiting Jersey in 1954 enjoyed a game of holiday cricket with makeshift wickets at St Brelade's Bay. The bay rejoices in a superb stretch of sand affording safe bathing at all states of the tide and a fine walking surface. The photograph also shows Fret Point, the bold cliff background to the bay. On the east are the Martello towers. These holiday-makers may have been staying at St Brelade's Bay Hotel, whose resident and manager was Mr D.J. Brecknell. In those days terms were from 51s per day with special rates for under-7s. Set in semi-tropical gardens with a heated swimming pool, this hotel was in the same family for five generations. No doubt its paddling pool, play area and 9-hole putting green would also appeal when interest in cricket on the beach waned.

General Boulanger's House, 1902.

General Boulanger's House was photographed in 1902 by Albert Smith, a photographer who commenced business in 1894. At different times he had premises in Beresford, Bath and Broad streets. The general escaped to Jersey from France to reside at Chateau des Roches opposite Hôtel L'Horizon at St Brelade's Bay about 100 years ago when Jersey was a haven for political refugees. The chateau was built in 1882, landscaped by an Italian architect and ordered by Parisian curio merchant, Jules Varnier. Greek temples, Roman altars, statues and fake antiques filled the bay and gardens. Varnier leased his home to the general who, between 1899 and 1891, could be seen 'pacing the sands surrounded by conspiritorial Frenchmen waving plans which always ended up in smoke.' The general epitomised France's patriotic fervour for a leader who would restore the monarchy and empire. Pictures of him on his famous black horse Tunis were plastered around Paris and a song composed: 'He Will Come Back', which was what the authorities feared, for the Boulangists were a strong party with 3 million francs of Royalist money behind them. Fate, however, took a hand. His mistress, Marguerite de Bonnemains, whom he worshipped, was found to be dying of tuberculosis. Disappointing his followers, he put Marguerite before his country and together they arrived in Jersey in October 1889. She died in July 1891 and within two months the distracted General Boulanger blew out his brains. His former home was eventually converted into flats. Stone foundations and iron statues remain but the fabric of the pretentious building is fast rotting away. Clemenceau said of Boulanger, 'He was indeed the handsomest straw-man France has ever seen.'

The Caesarea, 1960s.

The *Caesarea* entering St Helier Harbour in the 1960s with holiday-makers was contining a tradition of holiday sea transport which became echoed in the advertisement 'Night and day we are the one.' British Channel Island Ferries offered year-round, night out, day back sailings from Portsmouth and summer sailings, day out, night back from Weymouth. Modern, spacious ships with well-equipped cabins provide an outstanding service to Jersey and the Channel Islands. The fame of John Nettles in beckoned thousands to the 'sun-blessed' island, but its variety: 50 miles of marvellous coastline, history and cosmopolitan air have proved perennial for a century's holiday-makers and for those with an eye to its unique surroundings. Gerald Durrell, conservationist associated with the Jersey Wildlife Preservation Trust set up in 1963, acquired 30 acres of a sixteenth-century estate at Trinity to turn into a zoo, opened in 1959, where endangered species could be bred. An earlier discoverer and explorer, Henri Mouhot, who roamed jungles in Siam and Cambodia and discovered a forgotten civilisation, settled in Jersey in 1856, devoting all his time to the study of birds and shells before going off on his travels again with his brother who shared an interest in the making of daguerreotypes. The brothers both married English women, descendants of the explorer Mungo Park. By this early form of photography they aimed to record works of art from all over the world. Henri was honoured by the Royal Geographical Society. He died of jungle fever in 1861. Writing to his wife in Jersey he said, 'I experience a degree of contentment which I have never known before.'

Lillie Langtry.

The Royal Channel Islands Yacht Club's first lady member was the actress Lillie Langtry. From an early age world-famed for her beauty, she became a friend of Edward VII and of the many illustrious people of her day. She was born in 1853 at the rectory attached to the twelfth-century St Saviour's Church where her father, Dean Le Breton, was rector. Her first marriage was not happy. As soon as she came to London Oscar Wilde wrote a poem about her, and among countless admirers, great painters like Millais, Leighton and Whistler committed her to canvas. But 'the Jersey lily', as she was known, loved no place more than her own island. She was remarried at her father's church, St Saviour's, and at her request buried there after her death in 1929. A marble bust of her above her grave is now the only reminder of her fabulous beauty, but older residents recalled their grandparents' memories of 'the clergyman's beautiful daughter'.

She loved travelling in America, owned a ranch in California, a magnificent steam yacht and was able to hire the Prince's Theatre, London, specially for her appearance in *Antony and Cleopatra* in 1890, as portrayed in this photograph. However, her cottage Merman in St Aubin's Bay drew her back to Jersey whenever possible.

The Needle Rock, Plémont.

This dramatic 1912 photograph of the Needle Rock at Plémont with visitors alongside gives an idea of scale in pinnacle and cave. 'The view seawards from the large cave with the long pointed Needle Rock outside is very pleasing,' was how one famous guidebook described this scene. From the cave in the photograph Waterfall Cave could be reached and a series of others at low tide. Cliff paths in abundance (to Grand and Petit Becquet and Creux Gabourel) abounded in foxgloves, sea holly, michaelmas daisies, gorse, campion and thrift, but the Dolmen of Geonnais marked on older maps is no longer to be found. All over the Channel Islands it would appear that in the past, stones from dolmens have been used to build houses, barns and walls. Some islanders believe such plundering brings an attendant curse and the story is told of Sir Richard La Haye, a Norman knight who destroyed a cromlech and was thereon pursued with ill luck although he gave his house to the church in appeasement.

Decorations abound for the royal visit in 1921.

This interesting photograph from July 1921 shows the premises of Voisin & Co., King Street and New Street, decorated for the royal visit of King George V and Queen Mary, accompanied by Princess Mary. From Voisin's could be purchased 'Jersey's choicest souvenirs'.

'The house for novelties of charm and distinction' with beautiful shop window displays was a great draw for visitors, from where most of them purchased their allowance of Larbalestier's eau de cologne 'made in sunny Jersey'. Voisins carried an alluring display of cut-glass scent bottles together with lavender water in elegant royal blue and grey stoneware jars. 'Welcome to our King and Queen', the sign above the shop frontage muffled in swags, garlands and flags, was echoed all round the island. Adjoining Voisin's main building was Gaudin's, well-appointed tea rooms where French pastries were made on the premises. A. de Gruchy and Co., King's Arcade, the oldest drapery and house furnishing establishment in the Channel Islands, established 1814, was a worthy rival also offering novelties and souvenirs.

Royal Hotel, *c.* 1912.

Bree's Royal Hotel in David Place was run in conjunction with Main's Elfine Hotel, Gorey, at the time of this photograph, *c.* 1912. The Royal's telephone number, which was simply 8, kept ringing, for its excellent cuisine was famed. There were private sitting rooms, sumptuous lounges, bathrooms, a billiard room and 100 bedrooms. Competition was evidently growing throughout Jersey to attract holiday-makers and businessmen. The Halkett, first-class commercial and family hotel, sent the hotel porter to meet boats. Offering 'special terms to commercials', the licensed Stag's Head at Snow Hill, under the personal supervision of Arthur W. Parker, had a roof verandah and modern sanitation, while the Grand at Jersey, open all year, with a magnificent ballroom, central heating and its own orchestra, considered itself the premier and most up-to-date hotel of the Channel Islands. Summer terms were 18*s* 6*d* a day, and winter 15*s* 6*d*. Prolonged visits merited special terms.

Portelet Farm, 1900.

Portelet Farm at St Brelade's, which had become a guest house by the 1900s, was one of the oldest houses on Jersey. Miss Alice Mason, proprietress, advertised it as being in one of the finest positions on the island, offering French cooking, every comfort for visitors, private road to the beach and only 20 minutes from St Aubin's station. Boats were met on request and motor wagonettes were available for excursions round the island. Cycling and camping were becoming more popular and Miss Mason had an area set aside for visitors under canvas. At Portelet was also the Jersey Holiday Camp for men, women and family parties: 'bathing from own tents, tennis, wireless, . . . the healthiest and most enjoyable way to spend a holiday on Jersey.'

Old houses of the Channel Islands, such as Portelet Farm, traditionally had a stone plaque above the doorway, bearing the initials of the couple who had built them and the year, with possibly a heart motif as an emblem of their love.

St Aubin, 1904.

During construction of the first Jersey railway running round St Aubin's Bay an inhabitant raised the ancient 'Clameur de Haro' against trespass. Immediately this was investigated, to the benefit of the caller, who had to fall on his knees in the presence of a witness, calling, 'Help, my Prince, they are wronging me,' thus invoking a right almost 1,000 years old.

This photograph of St Aubin, dating from the early years of the twentieth century, shows the railway line in the foreground and the well-wooded bay. On the right of the photograph, standing in its own grounds with a palm lawn, 100ft above sea level, the Somerville Hotel commanded fine views of the curve of the bay. At the corner of a road opposite Bel Royal station a little further along the line, Maison Charles, a small house in which Charles II was said to have hidden, was pointed out to visitors.

St Catherine's Bay.

La Collette.

Bonne Nuit Bay.

The arrival of the Southampton boat and the bustle on Victoria Pier, *c*. 1909.

In the top photograph, taken in about 1909, we see the arrival of the Southampton boat. The St Malo boat and the Granville boat also docked here. At right angles to Victoria Pier was the Lifeboat House on the corner of what was then called the Old Pier.

As ships emerged from the harbour entrance there was a fine view of Elizabeth Castle with its long, straight slipway running up to the Grand Hotel on the Victoria Avenue Promenade and Esplanade. The lower photograph shows the bustle on Victoria Pier in 1909. It was said in the 1890s: 'The many charms of the Channel Islands are not sufficiently known to be appreciated at their proper value by holiday seekers, yet Jersey, practically a foreign land to the Londoner, is reached by steamer from Plymouth in one night.'

The States Chamber, Jersey Court House, 1926.

From the twelfth to the end of the seventeenth century a thatched building served as the Jersey Court House, until a newly erected building, enlarged and repaired in 1886, came into being situated on the south side of Royal Square. It was reported in 1925: 'The public may attend the Court while sitting. All proceedings are in French . . . . Before the President is a silver gilt mace presented by Charles II as a proof of his royal affection towards the Island of Jersey in which he had twice received in safety when excluded from the remainder of his dominions.' This beautiful mace, considered the sixth grandest in quality of all maces, was always carried before the Bailiff. In the corner of the court was kept an ancient relic, the prisoners' iron cage.

The Jacobean interior of the States Chamber, shown in this photograph from the 1920s, has a horseshoe form of three-tier seating. Since 1900 members have had the option of speaking in either English or French, though French was the official language. A tablet placed in 1920 was a reminder that Walter Raleigh was Governor of Jersey from 1600 to 1603 and on special occasions, a guard of halberdiers bearing halberds from Raleigh's day is on duty. The Bailiff's throne is placed 7 inches higher than that of the Lieutenant Governor by his side.

Agricultural labourers, St Mary, 1890s.

Six horses could be seen drawing the old metal ploughs in Jersey fields in the 1890s, the strongest two being placed immediately in front. The whole family with hired hands worked together in the open at harvest time, the oldest or youngest carrying out refreshments to help the work along. Potato digging was most important; 120lb barrels called centals were loaded onto flat carts and hauled off to market or harbour by strong horses. At Le Tapon Farm, St Saviour, in 1916, as many as thirty-two farm workers gathered, potato barrels for export being packed with straw and willow. No sooner had the potato crop been despatched than the future tomato season had to be attended to.

This photograph, copied from one of Kate Briggs' collection, is of St Mary Parish and shows the overseer among part of his workforce in the 1890s.

Harvest of the sea was carried out using long, heavy carts with slatted sides through which the sea water could drain. Piled high upon the carts, the rich seaweed was pulled by two horses, from Le Pulec, St Ouen – the best area for gathering it.

Visitors to Jersey, early 1900s.

This Southport family who loved the Channel Islands stayed at Breganze Boarding Establishment in Don Road, where windows were fitted with shutters, 'situated close to the sea, tennis courts and bathing pool – picnic parties daily, separate tables, terms moderate, under personal supervision of Mrs C. Clothier, Proprietress.'

A prize medal-winning photographer took this of the Hooleys, with Matilda on the right, a friend of my relative Kate Briggs from the slipper factory days in the Rossendale Valley. What the little girl with the lovely hair and her brothers were called I do not know. Sailor suits or Norfolk jackets and knickerbockers were popular for boys, lace-frilled dresses and boots for girls. As Kate used to say, the Hooleys were 'in good doings' but above all they were a loving family and it shows.

The Breganze in Don Road is listed with others having boarding terms of 10*s* a day for double rooms, and 12*s* 6*d* for single rooms.

The *Roebuck* beached, 1911.

Roebuck and *Reindeer* joined the GWR's Channel Island service in the 1890s, like the *Courier*, carrying thousands of trippers. Another caller at Jersey was *Princess Ena*, once the largest steamer owned by the London and South Western Railway Company. She carried Jersey's mail and had a chequered career, finally being burned out at sea off La Corbière. Rocks at Minquier and Paternoster had already been downfalls which she survived, but in 1935 Captain Lewis and his officers on board the Southern Railway steamer *Ringwood* saw *Princess Ena* sink below the waves for the last time. Another total loss in shipping was that of *Ribbledale* in 1926, bound for Jersey on a rough passage. Arriving at Bouley Bay, she anchored outside Ronez but dragged anchor in the gale and landed on rocks.

The photograph shows *Roebuck*, which in fog on 19 July 1911, became wedged between Les Kaines rocks.

Tomato pickers, early twentieth century.

At the time of this photograph the foremost crop on Jersey was the early potato. Farmers gave up nearly everything else to concentrate on this so that great quantities were exported. All the loads passed over the St Helier weighbridge and statistics kept at the office reported a record year in 1907, when 77,800 tons were shipped out of Jersey. In June that year the office did not close for a week. In 1920 the growers received £1,191,904, but the second crop of potatoes was usually consumed on the island unless very high prices could be fetched elsewhere.

Tomatoes were the crop second in importance, most being produced in the open, as old photographs show. 10,046 tons of tomatoes were exported from Jersey in 1923, apples, pears and large muscat grapes also being sent off to London. The photograph shows Jersey tomatoes being sorted and graded. Many hands were needed for this work in which speed was of the essence in order to ensure freshness, work now controlled by the Tomato Marketing Board.

Jersey Theatre, 1900.

The bold word 'Theatre' blazoned on the gable end in this photograph from the turn of the century is a reminder that Lillie Langtry appeared in the first production of *The Degenerates* at the Opera House, Gloucester Street, St Helier. The London Players appeared there in 1925. Old Jersey street scenes reveal details of brands, clothes, fittings, styles, customers and shopkeepers better than any description in a book. Examples are: Au Planteur in King Street, run by G. Barre, a shop wholly given over to tobacconist's wares and displays; Le Quesne, wine merchant, which sold Robertson's and Thorne's whisky, a white-coated manager and four assistants handling barrels, wooden cases and bottles stacked almost to ceiling level and many sizes of beautiful, natural stoneware jars of home-brewed beer; Gellender's Boot Store at 9 Beresford in the early 1900s stocked K Boots, a display of hundreds in its windows; the Beresford Library in the 1890s was kept by C. Le Feuvre, a very good printer whose window was plastered with examples of pasteboard cards and posters. The library was staffed by Messrs Sweeney and Du Parc, with two lady assistants clad from head to foot in black bombazine beneath a large notice 'Victoria College and General School Book Depository'. Copper plate printers in 1892 numbered six in the capital, having distinction above ordinary typesetters, Professors of Dancing, French, German and Music, governesses, saddlers, sailmakers and sawyers each with his own distinctive establishment, set a clear picture of the times as does a list of almost thirty milliners and dressmakers.

St Lawrence potato diggers, *c.* 1902.

This group from the turn of the twentieth century represents the labour force at a St Lawrence farm bordering the parishes of St John and Trinity. The travelling photographer would be busy at harvest time recording groups like this which was on the occasion of a successful end to potato lifting. In the summer of the German occupation my brother John Charles Houghton worked on such a farm before heading off to study Music at college, escaping only in the nick of time with hundreds of other Jersey residents. I vividly remember the family joy when he turned up on our doorstep, thin and sunburned, as we did not expect to see him again. Vivid too were his accounts of abandoned cars and personal goods as people fled to the harbour to crowd into hopelessly overloaded boats making for England.

During the potato season, each evening Victoria Avenue or The Esplanade was filled with hundreds of wagons and carts coming in from the country, almost blocking the 60ft roadway, the barrels being put on board steamers by a crane lifting sixteen tubs at a time.

Le Hocq Tower, 1938.

This photograph shows Le Hocq Tower in St Clement's Bay, and the dangerously spectacular rocks in line with the tower, which were a threat to shipping. 'I stayed at your hotel a couple of days on my way to Jersey' wrote Auntie Eva, who had needed only two halfpenny stamps to send this message from Bournemouth to her niece Miss Shankley, who lived in Blackpool. Both had shared the delights of the Channel Islands. It would appear that in the summer season the trusty old paddle steamer, SS *Bournemouth Queen* made passages to Jersey.

SS Bournemouth Queen.

Havre-des-Pas, early 1900s.

This image reveals some interesting fashions in adults' and children's clothing, and also street furniture. Note baby's bassinette and push chair! Deckchairs and sandcastle making were even then in vogue.

The paddle-steamer Emperor.

A happy crowd of day trippers disembarking from *Emperor* on 2 August 1928. This paddle-steamer was sighted off one of the 'magic isles'. All are wearing hats, flat caps, coats, etc. so different from a crowd on holiday eighty years later! No money for holiday gear in 1928!

PART TWO

Guernsey

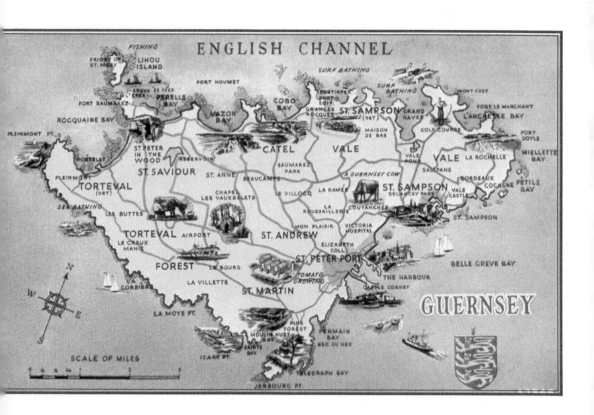

St Peter Port as it would have looked in the nineteenth century.

This artist's impression of St Peter Port with Bucktrout's shop on the left dates from the time of the Guernsey can used for carrying milk from the famous Guernsey cows. These traditional vessels can be seen in the photographs of the Guernsey butter churner (page 82) and the milkers on Sark (page 107).

The first red post box on the island, placed there by the novelist Anthony Trollope in 1853 when he worked for the Post Office, is still to be seen in Union Street but nowadays all post boxes on Guernsey are blue. Approach by sea to this picturesque town, at least 1,000 years old, has lost none of its magic. Cobbled streets and steep steps wander upwards between buildings that appear to be perched on each other's rooftops. Yachts, fishing smacks, cargo steamers and locally built schooners can still be seen in the magnificent harbour, but in the eighteenth century the harbour was crowded with private warships built at Havelet, La Piette and Les Baraques, which provided Guernsey with its then chief industry – privateering.

Tomatoes and tourism busied islanders after the Second World War, but since then tourism has boomed; 35,000 visitors arrive annually and some of the very wealthy have settled permanently to bask in sunshine and enjoy the low rates of taxes. With the exception of St Andrew, all ten of Guernsey's parishes have a sea border. Freedom from British import duties helped the island to develop as a commerical centre from the eighteenth century onwards.

Saumarez Park Bazaar, 1907.

Photographed in July 1907, the group of thirteen ladies represent the Scottish Stall at Saumarez Park Bazaar. Guernsey ladies, dressed in bonnets, velvet berets, tartans and with two sporrans in evidence, are backed by a 'crofter's farm'. This most interesting photograph, with which living descendents may well identify, would repay a recording of names for Guernsey local history.

James Saumarez was born in 1757 in St Peter Port in the house which became the Queen's Hotel. Coming from a family of fighting sailors, he joined the Navy at thirteen. In 1801 he was made a Rear Admiral, having fought at St Vincent and the Battle of the Nile. In the same year he defeated a Franco-Spanish fleet twice the size of his own. He died in Guernsey in 1836 and the De Saumarez Monument, erected in 1876 on Delancey Hill, commemorates this famous sailor, as does the holding of the bazaar.

The RMS *St Julien* off Guernsey, 1930.

The Royal Mail Ship *St Julien* photographed here off Guernsey, the island which old Norman writers called Grenezey or Green Isle, 1930s. Second in importance of the Channel Islands, it is roughly triangular in shape and at that time had a population of 38,000. From the boat, visitors were delighted with sightings of the thickly wooded cliffs enclosing Moulin Huet Bay, Saints Bay and Petit Bot Bay in the south. There were frequent trips to Jersey, Sark, Alderney and Herm; less frequently to St Malo and Cherbourg.

The *St Julien* is probably travelling from Weymouth or Plymouth. The Hare Steamship Company maintained a regular service between Plymouth, Jersey and Guernsey, and the St Malo and Binic Steamship Company had a boat running between Guernsey and St Malo, with offices at White Rock and North Esplanade. Nowadays large Sealink vessels enter St Peter Port, conveying visitors from Portsmouth and Weymouth on the mainland.

St Peter Port Coal Quay, 1900s.

This detailed postcard from the early 1900s shows the Victoria Hotel on the left, an old-time sailing ship and the stone memorial on the Coal Quay commemorating the visit of Queen Victoria and Prince Albert on 24 August 1846. The message sent by a visitor in April reads, 'This is where we landed . . . the coast much wilder than Jersey and it is beautiful to see fields of tulips and other flowers.'

The stone pier built in the thirteenth century survives as the Albert Pier, but in Elizabeth I's reign it was improved and by the time of Queen Anne the North Pier was built, enclosing the Old Harbour. The royal visit gave names to these two piers, in the Victoria and Albert yacht marina. The New Harbour was made because the original port was inadequate, drying out at low tide. In the 1920s the jetty provided more berths for fishing vessels and ferries. On St Julian's Pier is a memorial to the twenty-nine islanders who were killed in a German air raid.

The Upper Walk, St Peter Port, 1900s.

This splendid photograph from the 1900s at St Peter Port shows Castle Cornet in the background, and the extremity of the northern breakwater known as the White Rock, where the GWR and Southern Railway and Alderney steamers arrived and departed. As can be seen, crowds gathered along St Julian's Pier to White Rock to watch the shipping of thousands of tons of tomatoes, grapes and flowers despached daily in summer. The breakwater adjoining the castle, known as South Esplanade, is also visible in this photograph. The harbour had an area of 73 acres, but trade vastly expanded in the 1920s and '30s, requiring more berths. On the southern breakwater a large basin was popular for model yachting. Signals were displayed from the castle to notify the arrival and departure of mail boats and steamers.

The Old Harbour in the 1880s.

This photograph of St Peter Port from over a century ago gives another view of the Victoria Hotel and the many interesting buildings clustered around the Old Harbour; Hotel de L'Europe and Gargarth's Albion Hotel, not to mention an elegant, two-masted sailing ship. At the head of the harbour a copper statue of Prince Albert arrayed in robes of the Order of the Garter was erected on a granite pedestal 17ft high after the royal visit. Behind the statue is the town church, one of the oldest in the Channel Islands. At this time market stalls were laid out containing very large crabs, crayfish, lobster and conger eels, the latter in writhing heaps on marble tables. The old town was composed of narrow, steep streets rising from sea level to villas, gardens and the Arcade, above which was the Guille-Alle Library, opened in 1882 with 60,000 volumes. The library was instituted by two Guernsey men aiming to increase literacy among the islanders.

The Albert Statue, St Peter Port.

Another view of the Quay and Albert Statue at St Peter Port gives a close-up of more hotels that had appeared by the early 1900s. By the time this photograph was taken A. Haize ran the Albion Hotel; the People's Café was a large establishment and F. Stroubant's wines and spirits store had sprung up alongside. The ancient tram with open staircase advertises Neave's Food.

The Church of St Peter Port is first mentioned about 1048 in a charter of Duke William, Prince of Normandy. The oldest portion of the building is the nave, which dates from the thirteenth century. In 1913 a new peal of bells was placed in the church in memory of the rector who had died a year earlier. The old colours of the First Royal Guernsey Light Infantry Militia were placed in this church in 1887 and on the north side is the flag from the Alsatian flagship of the 10th Cruiser Squadron under the command of Admiral Tupper. Most interesting, close to the west door is the monument to the memory of Admiral Lord de Saumarez, who established the remarkable record of fighting and winning a battle against the French not far from his own home.

St Peter Port and Castle Cornet, 1893.

In 1893, the year of this photograph, St Peter Port was written of as follows: 'The first place the steamers from England call at is St Peter Port, the capital of the island, which has an excellent pier where the steamers moor at all states of the tide. It is situated on the slopes of eminence bordering the eastern coast. Between the town and the sea is an esplanade 150ft wide with a massive sea wall of granite stretching 2,500ft from north to south.'

Connecting Castle Cornet with the land is the castle breakwater shown in the photograph; 1,900ft long, 20ft wide and 15ft above the highest tides. Castle Cornet was founded in 1150, an important stronghold until 1672 and also residence of Governors of the Island. It was captured three times by the French, the first occasion in the reign of Edward I when the fortress had run short of provisions.

St Peter Port and the islands, 1902.

St Peter Port, the capital of Guernsey, can be seen here in 1902 as a well-built town of stone houses and villas, with fine public buildings and churches. The islands in the distance are Herm, Jethou and Sark. The harbour, with its excellent vantage point for spectators, was by the 1920s the scene of an annual regatta which took place in August. Guernsey's other port, St Sampson's, about 2 miles north of the capital, was connected to it by electric tramway, the fare 3d, every 12 minutes on weekdays. Granite quarries close beside the harbour exported enormous tonnage annually.

St Sampson's Harbour of 22 acres has an interesting namesake, St Sampson being patron saint of Guernsey. He was Bishop of Dol and the Channel Islands and previously of St David's in Wales, from where he fled to escape the Saxons in 554. He converted the inhabitants of Guernsey to Christianity and was said to have banished all moles, toads and serpents from the island. It is said that many of the fine Georgian and Regency buildings in the photograph were built from the spoils of smuggling and privateering, the latter referred to by the islanders as 'Free Trade', and making many fortunes.

The view from Fort George.

Fort George, only a mile distant from the Church of St Peter Port via Havelet Road, dates from 1782 and was termed fifty years ago as 'the one modern stronghold on the island', built to protect St Peter Port from naval attack. The Bailiwick of Guernsey, which includes Alderney, Sark, Herm and Jethou, is self-governing with a tradition of spirited independence, making its own laws and imposing its own taxes (4s in the pound when this photograph was taken in the early 1960s). Guernsey also mints its own currency and the ancient Norman-French patois used over many centuries still survives in outlying communities.

This comparatively small community achieved an impressive piece of construction work in a reservoir covering 38 acres and holding 240 million gallons of water, beneath whose surface lie seven farmhouses and 600 trees. A seawater distillation plant was also opened in 1960, producing 500,000 gallons per day.

Albecq looking towards Cobo, *c.* 1938.

Cobo and Albecq via Rohais could be reached at the time of this photograph by frequent motor bus services running in connection with the tramway. Among the many suggestions on how to spend a wet day in Guernsey was, 'For those who care to brave the elements a visit to Cobo, should half a gale from the west or south be blowing, can be recommended.' The Guernsey coastline is spectacular and the rocky nature, as can be seen from the photograph, combined with high seas would be well worth a cautious visit. The pools of Cobo were noted for their brightly coloured anemones on such calm days as the one portrayed in about 1938. Among the large, granite rocks in the vicinity, one resembling a lion's profile was pointed out to visitors.

Clifton Steeps, 1905.

The high flight of Clifton Steeps, St Peter Port, has people carefully posed upon it in the early 1900s, the photographer's art producing a beautiful picture expressive of this, the most ancient town in the Channel Islands. Guernsey was a staging post in the wine trade, visited by ships from England and the Mediterranean as a place of refuge or refuelling. Several great vaults and wine cellars where wine was left to mature are still there to serve as reminders of this busy industry. Its roadstead, protected by nearby islands, was popular with mariners and traders, but its beginnings must have been as a small fishing village. Old photographs of scenes like this and indeed of the rocky foreshores of Guernsey are reminiscent of Cornish villages, such as Polperro.

Elizabeth College, 1902.

Queen Elizabeth I was indeed the founder of this college in 1563, although this structure, imitation Tudor in style of architecture, dates from 1826. The Lower School was in Queen's Road and its playing fields in King's Road and Foote's Lane on the way to Cobo. The photograph dates from 1902, the college being one of a number of impressive buildings in New Town, south of Grange Road, St James's Street and Queen's Road where Government House stands. As is customary, the Union Jack flies whenever the Lieutenant Governor is in residence. Mount Row at its western end has a wooded valley with Havilland Hall standing in beautiful gounds, formerly the home of the Bluchers who once lived on Herm.

Vazon Sands and Fort Hommet, 1913.

Detachments from Fort George came for target practice to Fort Hommet situated on the promontory between Vazon Bay and Cobo Bay. Almost 400 yards beyond the track leading to the fort was Lion Rock, which I have previously mentioned. These young visitors on 6 August 1913 are much more interested in the old pastime of making sandcastles and forts decorated with shells, seaweed, lobster claws and other fascinating detritus from the rock pools nearby.

Referred to nowadays as Fort Houmet, the structure is about 220 years old. Damaged by shelling from British aircraft in 1944 during the German Occupation, it was considerably restored in 1982. The red rocks of the headland are vivid, lit by the rays of a sinking sun after a perfect Guernsey summer day. The soldiers stationed at Fort George on the cliff top used to dive from the rocks, bathing in the deep, clear water and held parades on the sands, leading it to become known as Soldiers Bay.

Guernsey street scenes, 1900 and 1949.

More young people, an old man with a hand cart, and a graceful iron bracket lamp are seen in the left-hand photograph of another narrow, ancient street in the capital of Guernsey, with Conron House showing at the bottom of the slope, *c*. 1900.

Although progress has brought modern shopfronts, the vigilance of the States Island Development Committee has prevented too much bad taste and depredation. As mercantile ventures succeeded and wealth accumulated, some of the medieval buildings became rich town houses, humble cottage premises developed into shops and the town generally expanded. A hospital was built in 1742 and Castle Cornet ceased to be the island prison, for a successor was built in St James's Street soon after 1811 with a subway linking it to the Royal Court House. The right-hand view of Pollet Street from 1949 shows little significant change.

The High Street, late 1960s.

This photograph from the late 1960s shows further building change in the island's streets. On the left is a branch of the well-known chain store chemists, Boots. The automobile, GBG 3770, further down signifies a well-entrenched system of car registration, this model quite a leap forward from the gentleman's hand cart in the photograph on page 78. A crowded High Street reveals possibly a busy Saturday, with the now less familiar sight of a police constable giving information to a passing visitor.

The writer of the card has an unusual report on a Guernsey Christmas Day: 'It is snowing here at the moment,' also another sign of advancing times, 'we had a very calm flight.' Half way up High Street and beyond the entrance to the Arcades, the Guernsey Savings Bank, still in its medieval setting, had appeared, Steep Berthelot, leading to Clifton, an area of elegant houses, retained many of its old buildings.

Guernsey fishermen, 1908.

Guernsey fishermen, with nets, baskets, sailing boat and other tackle make a splendidly nostalgic group, April 1908. These were the men who went out to catch the more delicate kinds of fish for the London markets. Reserved for Guernsey consumption were the large crayfish, big crabs and monster conger eels that the Channel waters supplied. The conger eels, especially esteemed in those days and for which a demand is returning, had to be fished for at night among the black reefs 15 miles away.

The men's traditional 'guernseys' were an obligatory part of seamen's clothing. By the seventeenth century knitting was the main industry, Elizabeth I encouraging knitting in Jersey and Guernsey to ensure the supply of knitted hosiery at court and also to discourage the male population from smuggling. A guernsey was worked in the round, each village having its own style passed down by word of mouth over generations.

The Fruit Market, St Peter Port, 1913.

H. Jackson, fruiterer and florist (wreaths and crosses made to order) had a splendid display in about 1913, with soft fruits and tomatoes carefully layered in tissue paper and a beautiful array of flowers. St Peter Port Market was formerly the Rectory Garden behind the church and was developed over many years. In 1780 the old Market Hall with the Assembly Rooms above was built, following a routine pattern, but in 1822 the Doric Market Hall was added. Still later and still more elaborate were the Victorian fish and meat markets.

Befitting a highly productive food area, marketing, with its abundant displays and bargaining appeal, remains a way of life, a visitor in 1847 calling it 'the grand object of the people's lives.' In 1800 the market was moved, but so congested was the area that New Market buildings were erected in 1882.

The market interior.

Butter making, 1917.

Butter making in Guernsey in 1917 had changed little from centuries before. Bowls, utensils and the churn itself are traditional and the farmhouse in the background is of great age. Farms and smallholdings produced tomatoes, new potatoes, grapes, peas, beans, melons, figs and cauliflowers. With glasshouses totalling 150 miles in length, Guernsey was once called the island of glass. Other products of the island were eau de cologne and tobacco. Edward Dupuy's high-class perfumery house, famous for 1868 Triple Extract Eau-de-Cologne, was situated at Commercial Arcade. Before 1914 quarrying of blue granite was most important.

In 1917 the laws for military service changed. All men capable of bearing arms, with the exception of chemists, pilots and Quakers, had been liable for service in the local militia. In 1921 the Royal Guernsey Militia was re-established upon a compulsory basis, but numbers were lower than they were before the First World War, thus releasing men for other occupations to assist the island's economy.

Guernsey calf in Cambridge Park, 1950.

Two small boys make friends with a gentle calf in Cambridge Park not far from St Peter Port in the 1950s. For many years the purity of the famous breed of Guernsey cattle has been carefully preserved. Regulations have forbidden the introduction of foreign strains since 1763. The Guernsey animal is larger and more hardy than the Jersey breed and its yellow and white distinguishing markings are quickly recognisable.

The Park, once known as New Ground, was renamed Cambridge after the Duke of that name visited Guernsey about 120 years ago. The massive 100ft Victoria Tower, another reminder of Queen Victoria's visit in 1846, is close to Cambridge Park.

A Guernsey citizen in 1917 invoked the ancient right of a Channel Islander by the 'Clameur de Haro'. He objected to the removal of elm trees from Cambridge Park. In the presence of witnesses he went on his knees crying, 'Help, my Prince, they are wronging me.' The matter has to be decided upon immediately, but any misuse of the cry, which goes back to the eleventh century, brings severe penalty.

A Bullock Plough, Guernsey.

Bullock plough, 1922.

This Guernsey bullock plough was photographed in 1922 in a rural setting of haystacks, fields and farm workers, which, but for the men's clothes, may well have looked the same a century or more before that. Bullocks, like horses, had to be shoed by the blacksmith in order to work for man. Their shoes were split because of their cloven hooves, unlike the horseshoe shapes of mares and stallions. Examples of both kinds of shoes, relics of the late nineteenth century and beyond, are preserved in folk museums. In the Plough Room, on view is one large plough used for a mixed team of oxen and horses. Bullock ploughs have turned up interesting and ancient remains in their time.

Traditional foods like the Gache or ormer were still eaten at the time of this photograph. The Gache, a fruit cake, is still sold by some confectioners and cafés. The ormer, a mollusc growing on the rocks, when in season was prised open, the flesh beaten and fried and the shells, with their beautiful mother of pearl linings, made into pretty mementoes.

An unknown wreck off Guernsey.

Of many wrecks off Guernsey the ketch *Iris* went aground in 1918 east of Fort la Marchant, the body of the Mate of the *Iris* being washed ashore at Fontenelle Bay. One survivor had managed to get ashore on an islet near Herm, making himself a shelter from wreckage and seaweed, but sadly, although in sight of passing ships, he perished unnoticed, only to be found a month after the wreck. The wrecking of a ship off Guernsey carrying botanical specimens resulted in the pretty Guernsey Lily. Bulbs washed ashore rooted in fertile soil. Accounts differ as to whether this lily is of South African or Japanese origin.

On Christmas Day 1982 a Roman wreck, since referred to as the *Asterix* was located off Guernsey by a skindiver. Where the Race and the Swinge meet many ships have been wrecked. There was no warning light until 1912 when Mannez, the Alderney lightship, was built with its 400,000 candlepower beacon and foghorn.

'How many vessels have been wrecked, how many lives lost, history can only partially record,' was written of this subject in 1924. The unknown wreck in the photograph, contemporary with the *Agilis* of Guernsey towards the end of the nineteenth century, is one of these, thought to be off Rocquaine Bay.

The Prince of Wales's yacht.

The Prince of Wales's yacht *Osborne*, 1882 was, on occasions, sighted off Guernsey. As the eldest son of Queen Victoria and her consort Albert, he had admired the Royal Yacht *Victoria and Albert* and desired a similar craft for himself. Known as a 'big spender' nothing was spared in the way of luxurious trappings within and without. He entertained his friends aboard the *Osborne*. Both yachts were photographed by A. Debenham of West Cowes.

The *Victoria and Albert* was used by the royal couple when they travelled to Balmoral for their long summer holiday.

For the 1898 Regatta, Edward, Prince of Wales ordered that *Osborne* should be moored in Osborne Bay, to serve as a private grandstand for his friends to watch the Cowes races.

Fruit baskets on the quay, 1911.

Fruit baskets on the quay at St Peter Port in 1911 bear witness to the chief sources of Guernsey's trade in those days. Guernsey was then supplying new indoor potatoes in winter and early spring when prices were high, but later outdoor potatoes at a popular rate. Guernsey tomatoes, quite different from Jersey, were all grown under glass, the early crops with artificial heat, the later under sun. They represented three-quarters of the produce exported. It was estimated that each season they filled three million baskets worth £1,500,000. Beans, melons and fresh figs also augmented exports. Small wonder that in those days Guernsey was described as 'a land of smallholdings', there being 2,000 growers with plots averaging 5½ acres.

As early as the fourteenth century, dried fish and agricultural products were taken back to Gascony in the ships that had brought wine for storage on the island.

Victor Hugo statue in Candie Gardens.

Jean Boucher's dramatic statue of the great French writer Victor Hugo (1802–85), standing on a granite mass, was erected in Candie Gardens gazing towards France. Self-exiled, he spent fifteen years on Guernsey, as a result of which, most of this prolific writer's work was done in the Channel Islands where he was as close as possible to his homeland.

Candie Gardens, especially the lower gardens, specialised in rare shrubs and flowers which flourished in the shelter of its mellow walls. Near the statue of Victor Hugo at the time of this postcard, but now gone, was a bandstand where musicians of the Royal Guernsey Militia gave concerts. The Modern Museum and Art Gallery houses many treasures of the past and regularly stages exhibitions. The former museum from which exhibits were transferred was the Lukis and Island Museum as the top of Cornet Street.

Maison Victor Hugo, Hauteville.

Victor Hugo was once the renowned tenant of Hauteville House, a large, double-fronted building about 250 years old. Fifty years ago it was possible to view daily from 10.30–12 p.m. and 2–6 p.m. 'except when the family are in residence'. The interior was then referred to as being like a museum with valuable china, dark oak furniture, tapestries, some by Gobelin, and leather work on walls and ceilings. Still open to the public and unchanged, it is now owned by La Ville de Paris.

Hugo lived here from 1855 to 1870. He wrote, always standing, in what he called his Lighthouse Room which commanded a panoramic view of Guernsey, whose shops were laden with fabulous antiques from the spoils of privateering. Hugo purchased and 'adapted' these according to his own tastes. He was also a painter, 350 of his pictures being on view at the Maison de Victor Hugo in Paris. Daily at 6 a.m. he took a cold shower after which he would write for five hours, followed by lunch, and in the afternoon he would walk miles round the island.

The Conservatory, Hauteville House, 1903.

Visitors were urged not to miss Hauteville House, one of the showpieces of St Peter Port, on account of its unique furnishings, some idea of which is given by this 1903 photograph of the interior, showing the conservatory, devoid of the dark, oak furniture the novelist concentrated on collecting. Basket chairs and bunches of cheerful marguerites make a pleasant, ligher contrast to Spanish leather, silk tapesteries and priceless china salt-cellars. One table in the house originally belonged to Charles II. The red drawing room contains relics from Louis XV and gilt figures from the Doge's Palace in Venice. In 1860 a special bed was ordered for the visit of Garibaldi who never arrived, so this large, heavy, carved oak piece of furniture remained unused. *Les Miserables* and *Toilers of the Sea*, the latter portraying the islanders among whom Hugo made his home, were written here.

Other authors inspired by the Channel Islands included Algernon Charles Swinburne, writer of ballads, Sir Gilbert Parker, Helen Wallace, D.K. Broster and M.E. Bradden. *The Great Leviathan* by D.W. Barker portrays scenes on Guernsey and Sark.

Victor Hugo returned to France in 1870 at the restoration of the Republic. The house remains as he left it, a remarkable time capsule.

Castle Cornet's main gate, 1960.

Castle Cornet was founded in 1150 in the reign of Henry II and is steeped in the island's history. In 1642 three Commissioners of Guernsey, Peter Carey, Peter de Beauvoir and James de Havilland were instructed to seize the Royalist Governor Sir Peter Osborne, but were themselves outwitted and imprisoned in Castle Cornet. They cut their way out of their cell into an adjoining area conveniently housing a store of cotton from which they made a rope and effected their escape. Sir Peter Osborne held out for the king until Admiral Blake forced surrender. Nearby Jersey had helped to provision the castle by fleets of small boats. For almost nine years it refused to yield, being the last stronghold in the British Isles to submit to the Puritans' Long Parliament.

In 1672 Castle Cornet was partially blown up when lightning struck the powder magazine. In the 1930s it was reported there were only five or six pensioners acting as caretakers and guides who occupied the castle. In 1945 George VI presented Castle Cornet to the people of Guernsey.

Victoria Tower and gardens, 1909.

This splendid folly was built to celebrate the royal visit of 1846, the order for its erection reading: 'A castellated tower, to celebrate the landing of the Sovereign and to serve as a telegraph station for Alderney and as look out for royal and other flags.' £2,000 was raised by public subscription, the site supposedly that of an ancient menhir, La Pierre L'Hyvreusle.

The gun in the 1909 photograph is inscribed: 'Presented to Her Majesty's Government to the island of Jersey as a trophy of the Russian War, 1856.' It was placed in the gardens of Victoria Tower near Cambridge Park. Visitors could climb the 100ft red stone tower, the key being kept at the fire station, a custom which continued, like the firing of the signal gun at noon from Castle Cornet. At the time of the German Occupation two guns from the gardens of Victoria Tower were hastily buried before the enemy arrived, said to be relics of the First World War. It seems likely that this gun from the Crimea was one of those buried in 1940 before German troops found them for melting down, a fate which befell other guns.

Underground Hospital, 1950s.

This entrance to the German Underground Hospital on Guernsey was photographed about ten years after hostilities ceased. In 1940 when German forces occupied the Channel Islands, thousands, including my brother, escaped in overloaded boats. Almost the whole population of Alderney left for Britain, but there was suffering, privation and death for some who stayed. Garrisons, minefields and bunkers despoiled the countryside, relics remaining today in gun emplacements and watch towers. Liberation Day, 9 May 1945, is observed annually on Guernsey and the island made a rapid recovery.

The former German Underground Hospital is located at La Vassalerie Road not far from St Andrew's Parish Church. It was built by slave workers of the Third Reich, many of whom were buried in the concrete as they perished excavating solid rock, 60,000 tons of which were removed. Tons of ammunition were stored here by the Germans, but the hospital proper was used for only six weeks.

Little Chapel of Les Vauxbelets.

This little chapel at Les Vauxbelets, Guernsey, has been of endless fascination to visitors and this photograph is particularly interesting as it shows the builder himself, Brother Deodat, standing with trowel in hand. Started in 1914, La Grotte was built by one of the brothers of a former religous house, De La Salle Order of Christian Schools, who continued his building until 1923. Modelled on Lourdes Grotto and composed of pottery, china and shells including those of the ormer, like the Shell House on the Isle of Wight it continues to be added to and is a more powerful attraction than the nearby Church of St Andrew of the Sloping Orchard, a small, ancient foundation. Also in this parish is the Chapel of Christ the Healer, built in 1957 of granite, on Le Monnaie Road.

The Hostel of St John, Saumarez Park.

The Hostel of St John, Saumarez Park, Catel, is a home for the elderly, but at one time, when Guernsey had no official Government House, it became the residence of the Lieutenant Governor. Once the family seat of Lord de Saumarez in whose family it remained for 200 years, the property was enlarged in the early 1900s. The 4th Baron was connected with the Diplomatic Service and he brought workmen from Japan to erect Japanese-style buildings on the estate. Lord de Saumarez received the Prince of Wales in 1935 and in 1938 the estate was purchased by the States of Guernsey.

Of another Guernsey family, Captain Philip Saumarez had entirely different connections, dying in action, aged 37, sailing round the world with Anson in the *Centurion*. Saumarez Manor, an hereditary seigneurie and Norman manor house in the area of Fermain Bay, holds the voyage log which records a rich prize, the capture of a Spanish treasure ship.

Saints Bay from Loari Point, 1930s.

This small, charming inlet takes its name from the fact that the Archbishop of Rouen, banished from his diocese, landed on its shores. Two protruding rocks on the left of the bay, presumably from their shapes, became known as the Saints and are accessible from Smugglers' Lane, a path between high hedges. Saints Bay Picnic House supplied refreshments. Icart Common, covered with grass and furze, Icart Point, the most southerly headland in Guernsey, and Haut Nez, Guernsey's highest land, were all popular visiting places. The headland, reminiscent of Sark, with its little coupée, gives superb double views, Petit Bot Bay and Moye Point being on the other side.

The narrow road passing a Martello tower, seen on the left of the photograph, leads to a fishermen's harbour. A Seigneur of Blanchelande, who helped to pay for its construction, had his manor on this high ground and was commemorated by a granite obelisk, which the Germans uprooted when fortifying the haven.

Fermain Bay.

Nowadays in summer there is a half-hourly boat service to Fermain Bay from St Peter Port Harbour, the bay, like almost every bay in Jersey and Guernsey, having a round Martello tower. Situated at the bottom of a densely wooded glen, this shingly shore was always popular for bathing although many years ago ladies kept to the right, gentlemen to the left. Furze-covered cliffs soften the harsh, black rocks, Fermain meaning strong rock. Doyle's Monument, now termed Doyle Column, for the original 100ft tower has gone, the fishing haven of the Bec du Nez, the Pine Forest and Marble Bay are all in the vicinity of Fermain Bay. Three parallel lines close to where the monument was situated run to the edge of the cliff. Similar to ancient camps found on the British mainland, they are probably Celtic remains. These and traces of stone walling are all that is left of the Chateau de Jerbourg mentioned in ancient documents.

Moulin Huet Bay with the 'Dog' and 'Lion' rocks.

Another view of the lovely Bay of Moulin Huet taken in 1893, but showing in the distance the Doyle Monument, an Ionic column 96ft tall and 300ft above sea level. This was at Fermain Vale and erected to the memory of Sir John Doyle under whose Governorship the excellent military roads traversing the island were constructed. A spiral staircase to a square, railed platform could be ascended by visitors, the key to the monument being kept at a refreshment cottage on the Jerbourg road.

At that time it was said of Guernsey: 'The island is divided into three excursions made either in private carriages costing 20 shillings a day or in cars for each seat in which 2 shillings and 6 pence must be paid . . . being the trotting along narrow winding lanes down into deep valleys, careering through the commons by the summit of the cliffs, breathing the strong sea air or gliding along the flat shores of little bays bordered with golden sands and studded with rocks of fantastic shape.' From this point the Dog and Lion rocks are seen to best advantage.

An early visitor to Guernsey, the artist Pierre-Auguste Renoir, completed seventeen paintings during his stay on the island in 1883. His 'Children on the Seashore' has the setting of Moulin Huet Bay.

Steps to Petit Port beach.

This scene photographed in September 1954 shows the rocky Guernsey beach of Petit Port, one of many such in this part of the island. This little inlet where the sea was reported in the 1920s as 'bluest of blue' was accessible by 208 steep stone steps down an almost perpendicular cliff. Here was one of the best places to bathe for 'at low tide a fine stretch of firm sand is exposed and an abundance of rocky nooks and pretty caves provide dressing rooms.' Petit Port with its neighbour Moulin Huet were regarded as the most beautiful bays on the island. A cave leading to a 'chimney', a natural shaft between rocks, revealed ferns and ivy fringing the top.

At the most rugged part of Guernsey's coastline is Hanois Lighthouse, first lit in 1862. The name Hanois, meaning agony, reflects the great number of people drowned. La Table des Pions is another name evoking history, for pions were young men dressed in black caps and white blouses who ceremonially accompanied island dignitaries in their inspection of highways. Here, where the land ended, they traditionally took refreshment. Victor Hugo's graphic description of Hanois Rocks is 'this midnight assassin.'

Petit Bot Bay and valley.

In the 1900s when this photograph was taken, Petit Bot was regarded as one of Guernsey's best known inlets, very popular because of its beautiful approach by road, which near the bay entered a winding valley leading to the beach. Just above the beach a stream and mill were pointed out as a scene of crime over 100 years ago when thieves entered the mill and threw the old miller to his death out of a little window above the wheel. One of Guernsey's round towers is to be seen in the photograph. A cave on the west side was visited and cliff-top views in both directions recommended, the westerly steep cliff path leading to the grandest cliff scenery of all at Sommeilleuse Point and the Gouffre. This deep gulley between cliffs was where Mrs Guille slipped and fell to her death in the early years of the twentieth century. The name is associated with the Guille-Alle Library.

Jerbourg, 1892.

A scene at Jerbourg Point over a hundred years ago, giving a closer view of the Doyle Monument. The path around the Jerbourg Headland above Petit Port gave wonderful vistas of sea rocks, cliffs, flowers and sea birds, the Pea Stacks serving as nesting points. The Doyle Monument was destroyed by the Germans as it served as a landmark for their fortifications. An obelisk with a nearby viewfinder has since taken its place. Not far away is the inlet named Valley of Beasts, more usually called Telegraph Bay because of the cable which used to run from here to Jersey. The horse-drawn, wheeled cart with its large headlamps is a vanished gem from past times, but fortunately the abundant wild flowers, sand crocus, sea pink, wild thyme, spurge and gorse still return annually.

Cobo, 1900s.

This photograph of the roadway at Cobo, the same vintage as the previous image, also shows a charming wheeled vehicle, a horse-drawn landau in the early 1900s. Cobo stone was used for the Norman-style Church of St Matthew at nearby Vazon, which dates from 1854. It was inspired by a child, Marianne Carey, who persuaded her father to build a church for the fishermen and whose family raised nearly all the money required for its construction. Overlooking Cobo Bay is the Sentinel, a hill which now belongs to the States. Fir trees planted seventy years ago cover the ancient watch-house which gave this distinctive eminence its name. The watch-house was part of a defence chain against the French, fitted with a beacon ready to ignite. A siren was installed in 1939 which sounded the alert in 1940, the occasion of German bombing. Paths connect the Sentinel, otherwise known as Le Guet, with the coast road and Cobo, as shown in this photograph from a time when thoughts of war were not in mind.

Bordeaux Bay, *c.* 1950 and
St Sampson's Church, 1964.

Not far from Vale Castle, now a shell overlooking the entrance to St Sampson's Harbour, lies Bordeaux Bay, of special interest to zoologists, a fisherman's cove with interesting rock formation and great variety of marine life. The island shown is that of Hommet Paradis, mentioned in Victor Hugo's *Toilers of the Sea*. The hero Gilliat resided in a haunted house on the islet and eventually met his death on the dangerous rocks. Ruined Vale Castle was the main entrance of the Clos du Valle, a small island before Lieutenant Governor Doyle had it joined to the mainland.

Reviewing Guernsey churches, and especially St Sampson's, an interesting message came from a photographer and metal worker visiting Guernsey churches on behalf of the Victoria and Albert Museum, London. It reads, 'At St. Sampson's I have photographed the brass and other objects of base metal. Unfortunately my camera broke down and I have had to borrow one. The results may not be very good.' Pity the poor photographer!

Perhaps like my family and other visitors that summer of 1964 he would be comforted by the promise of Strawberry Farm, St Saviour's, where you could have 'viewing and tasting of freshly picked stawberries with Guernsey cream.'

A traditional Guernsey kitchen (above)
and water pump near St Sampson's (left).

As models for my father Clement Houghton in the late 1920s, my sister and I stood under minature cascades, wearing coal-scuttle sou'westers and oilskins, gathered flowers in woodland settings, leap-frogged over each other, scaled high boulders or, milk kits in hand, ran down lanes with the dogs. Likewise, twenty years earlier, this unknown Guernsey girl near St Sampson's is obliging some professional photographer by drawing a glass of 'water bright' from the pump, her white cat artistically placed in the foreground.

This may well have been seen from the train following the curve of Belle Grève Bay. The Guernsey Railway Company, incorporated in 1888, converted from steam to electric traction on this line, where previously locomotive *Shooting Star* and *Sampson* were among six 20hp machines used. The line closed down in 1934. Some inhabitants on Guernsey had never seen a train, but each cyclist had to be registered and exhibit a number plate obtainable from the constable's office.

The kitchen scene above is typical of a Guernsey cottage from the turn of the twentieth century, faithfully portrayed in the Saumarez Park exhibition of Rural Life and Crafts. Cooking pots, cast-iron pans, earthenware, willow-pattern plates, oil lamps, the black kettle in the fire grate with its handy kindling, the spindle-backed chairs and other authentic details express a way of life that persisted unchanged for centuries. This excellent photograph was published by Norman Grut of Guernsey.

PART THREE

Sark, Alderney & Herm

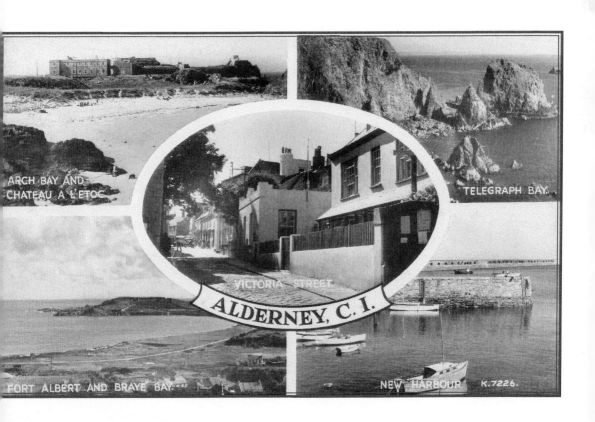

Dixcart Hotel, Sark, 1940s.

Dixcart, established around 1860, is the oldest hotel on Sark and has been visited by many famous people. It cost 8s to lunch there in the early 1960s, by which time hotels numbered five, with four guest houses. La Sablonerie, originally a farmhouse built almost 400 years ago, first opened in 1948. Sark lobsters were its speciality and the telephone number was easy to remember: Sark 61.

At the one post office, before parcel post was established, few letters arrived in the 1920s, but the steamer later brought bags of mail in summer. The densely wooded Dixcart Valley and Bay were included in twelve places listed in 1926 as 'some characteristic features of Sark'.

A rural scene, Sark, 1900s.

The traditional sun bonnet, milk can and placid, tethered cow continued unchanged for years. Not far from this scene was Mill Lane with its conical mill tower, the old mill built by the first Seigneur in 1571 on the highest point in the Channel Islands and in the direction of Little Sark. Where Little Sark is attached to Big Sark by La Coupée, it was reported that schoolchildren crossing in strong winds had to crawl on hands and knees, which I found reminiscent of a remote Cornish village where the children had to carry a heavy bucket with a big stone inside whenever they visited outside lavatories during similar tempestuous conditions, otherwise they would have been blown away.

Farming and dairy produce continue as main industries on Sark with tourism increasingly important. Stock's Hotel in Dixcart Lane, set in one of the valleys, the island's beauty spot, had its own farm with pedigree Guernsey cattle and a market garden.

Above: Old-fashioned transport on the Quay, Sark, 1937.
Below and left: Ponies and traps and coachman, John Selby.

The scene on the quay at Sark in 1937 shows the horse-drawn transport much relied upon as all motor vehicles have always been banned by law. A few tractors used for ploughing are mechanised but there was no tarmacadam on the roads when this Sark visitor wrote to America about 'living for ever in this peace, perfect peace'. These picturesque carriages were not allowed to run on Sundays except in such emergencies as when the Home Secretary visited Sark in June 1965.

The Archway of Jersey granite in the same photograph, dated 1588, gives a clue to the colonisation of Sark, which was brought about by Helier de Carteret of Jersey who petitioned Elizabeth I for the chance to do this, with forty-two fellow islanders, each of whom was allotted a tenement. Before 1550 Sark's history is vague.

The pony and trap depicted in the photograph above was much used to canter along the leafy lanes of Jersey and Guernsey but especially on the island of Sark where no motorised traffic was permitted. The photograph dates from about 1920. The accompanying photograph of John Selby, famous Sussex coachman (not a Jersey man) gives some idea of the dress and obligatory long whip used in early coaching days, long before the smart pony and trap.

The Mill, Sark, 1931.

Standing 365ft above sea level to catch wind force, the Mill at Sark was built by Helier de Carteret. A stone bears the date 1571 and the mill ground corn until 1919 for Seigneur and tenants. This beautiful photograph goes back to the days when the mill was functional and picturesque. German Occupation of the island used it as a look-out post and its sails fell into decay, although a weather-vane has survived. It is now a gift shop, but when a working mill, feudal rights would be attached. Mill soke meant that tenants must grind their corn there and no other mill could be built without permission. Dues for this privilege or duties were demanded by the feudal baron. The Seigneurie receives tithes on wool, lamb, minerals and corn.

Sark, like Alderney, is in the Bailiwick of Guernsey to where are sent cases with which the Sark authorities cannot deal.

Every man of more than one year's residence was required to give two days' free labour on the roads or to pay labourers' wages. In 1924 this amounted to 4s per day. A ruined windmill on the Hog's Back, the ridge between Derrible and Dixcart Bays, from where an extensive view could be had, was reported in a 1924 guidebook to Sark.

The Prison, Sark, 1920s.

This tiny prison on Sark has two cells and in the 1920s when the photograph was taken the lock was growing rustier year by year from disuse. G.R. Sims, who visited Sark even before that, reported amusingly on Sark's 'prison'.

'Some time ago a girl stole a pocket handkerchief and was sent to prison. The prison door had grown rusty from long disuse and would not open. When it did open it would not shut. The little girl was told to be good and stop there, but she set up such a dismal howl the women of Sark rushed out. They fetched their knitting and sat down in the prison with her and told her stories to pass the time. The next day, the girl walked out, went to the policeman's home and asked if she might go home if she promised never to steal again. He said he thought she might and the gaol has not had a single occupant since.'

In recent years it has been used for short-term offenders, more serious criminals being sent to Guernsey for trial.

NO. 882. CHURCH, SARK.

St Peter's Church, Sark, 1931.

In July 1931 St Peter's Church, whose bells are cast from field guns belonging to the Sark Militia, was photographed. Built in 1820, it has a clock tower and attractive unpretentious interior, with more recently, new, beautifully-worked hassocks. What was the old vicarage on Sark was also once the Seigneurie. Le Manoir, as it is called, a beautiful house, is now in private hands and the vicar lives opposite the church. Weddings, not frequent on Sark, are linked with tradition. The bride and groom travelled round the island, giving out cake and wine to mark the event. When a death occured all islanders had to be notified in similar fashion.

Traditionally the taverns were closed on Christmas Day while church services were held and after service the men all went off hunting and shooting until it was time to return for Christmas dinner.

Belief in witchcraft was widespread; ancient spells were used to banish illness and on Sark also may be seen the 'Witch's Seat' which every islander used to construct, jutting out from his chimney.

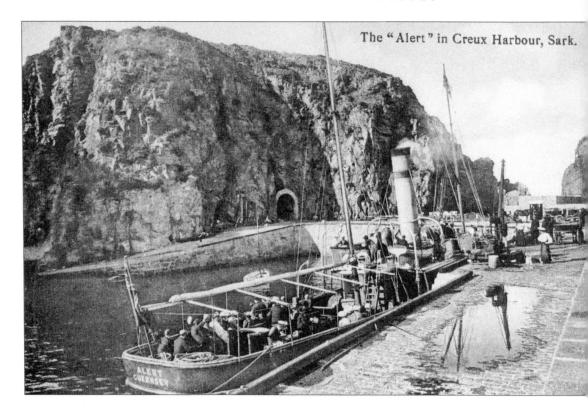

The "Alert" in Creux Harbour, Sark.

Creux Harbour, 1900s.

In the 1900s when this lovely photograph was taken, steamers like the *Alert* left Guernsey daily from White Rock at 10 a.m., the passage taking one hour. This timetable applied to July, August and September, moderated in other months, and the return boat left Sark promptly at 5 p.m., in winter at 3 p.m. The fare was 5*s*, returning same day; a mere 3*s* 6*d* if travelling one way. At low tide it was not possible to enter the harbour at Sark and landing was achieved by using small boats for which a charge of 6*d* was made. A poll tax was payable by all visitors over sixteen years of age.

The Alderney Steam Packet Company in Pollet Street was running the steamers in those days, but by the 1960s it was called the Commodore Shipping Company.

Creux Harbour, as can be seen from the photograph, is backed by almost perpendicular cliffs which enclose a cove with two short piers. It was built in 1570 and is thought to be the smallest harbour in the world.

Creux Harbour, 1894.

This photograph of Creux Harbour with its quays of red stone is over a century old. When it was taken, 'this charming little island of 1,274 acres' had a population of 580. It is interesting to discover that the fare from St Peter Port in those days was only 2s return. This century-old report refers also to the Buron rocks by Creux Harbour and 'a lofty mass of granite, Le Tas, rising boldly out of the sea', and the Pot, a deep hole down to the beach with which it communicates through a natural archway.

To the left of this archway two galleries had been opened in order to search for gold in a vein of quartz. Even earlier, in the 1840s, silver mining was tried out for the Sark Mining Company – it was the road to ruin. The Seigneur at that time, Ernest Le Pelley, had invested in the scheme and such was his loss, he had to transfer the Seigneurie to Mrs T.G. Collings from whom the Seigneur, Michael Beaumont, was descended.

Creux Road from the Tunnel, 1907, and Maseline Harbour, 1951.

The new, less beautiful, concrete Maseline Harbour close to Creux was constructed by 1949 with a more spacious quay. It was opened by HRH the Queen, then Princess Elizabeth, and Philip, Duke of Edinburgh, on their first official visit to Sark. Creux Harbour being much less used, landings made here are almost at the entrance of the tunnel hewn through the cliff. The photograph from 1907 shows the beginning of the steep climb beyond the tunnel, up the hill to Sark's only substantial settlement of houses and shops.

The new harbour cost £52,000, the sum being raised by the islanders. The steep hill in the top photograph towards La Collinette used to be called Vallée du Creux. The day visitor was directed to see Creux Derrible 'wonderful and awe-inspiring', the Pot, a similar creux, and an old stone cider mill, but 'the grandest and most wonderful scene in the Islands', they were told, was the Coupée. Sark Lighthouse is situated at Point Robert just before entering Maseline Harbour.

The Coupée, 1880.

The Coupée, a natural viaduct 260ft above sea level, uniting Great and Little Sark, is being gradually eroded by the sea, so the day may well come when the two will be separated. One marvels at the man leaning against a flimsy rail and no rail at all on the other precipitous side where the wagonette and horse are passing. The ribbon roadway is 300ft long and 6–8ft wide. A steep, risky track led down the eroded cliff from the slightly more gradual slope on the right to the Grande Grève, the most extensive beach on Sark and good for swimming. A report in 1922 read, 'It is a grand experience to stand on the Coupée in a gale; the wind nearly lifts you off your feet and the spray from below drenches like a tropical rain. Do not trust to the rails for support; they are not too firmly set.'

The Coupée was used as dramatic setting for 'Burnt', an episode of the popular *Bergerac* television series in which actor John Nettles appeared.

La Seigneurie, Sark, and its entrance.

The Seigneurie on Sark in the 1920s was open to the public on Mondays. An ancient monastery was founded on its site in about the year 565 by St Magloire but nothing of that remained. St Magloire's body was stolen from Sark to fulfil a condition laid down by a King of Brittany, that he would provide a monastery if the bones of a saint to place in it were obtained. In the 1920s there remained ivy-covered, Gothic-windowed outbuildings used as store rooms, and ponds where the original monks bred fish. Among small guns was one given by Elizabeth I to the Seigneur of Sark in 1572, Helier de Carteret, who established a loyal community on the island. La Seigneurie, 20 minutes' walk from La Collinette, is distinguished by its wrought-iron gates and gardens of semi-tropical plants laid out by Dame Sybil Hathaway. The house was begun in 1565 and enlarged in 1730 by the Le Pelley family. The Revd W.T. Collings, when he was Seigneur, built a signalling tower from which to contact Guernsey in emergencies. When the fine trees in the grounds began to block views from the signalling tower the reverend built a new tower rather than cut them down.

Arched rock, Dixcart Bay, 1909.

Dixcart Bay was very popular for its safe bathing, gently shelving beach and plenty of sand at low tide. It also offered great scope for cave exploration, having one of the longest on Sark. On the north side was this natural arch, photographed in 1909. Derrible Bay and the Hog's Back have more caverns under their cliffs. In 1960 a twelve-passenger boat called *The Triolet* did a five-hour excursion round Sark, visiting caves and beaches and making a special stop for refreshments, the whole trip costing 15s per person. Farm teas consisting of lobster sandwiches, strawberries and fresh cream were then a speciality at Plaisance Farm. On the way to the famed Venus Pool, which every visitor went to see, were La Moserie Tea Gardens which had an interesting well. Sark pastry cook, Denis Le Goubin, had a grand display of cakes at his shop, Le Carrefour.

Little Sark then had a population of twenty, exemplifying rural life with its tiny square of cottages, village pump and rough track leading to the fields beyond.

Les Autelets rocks, 1880s.

The coast of Sark shows some of the sea's most fantastic work. The Creux, like nearly all the caves and passages cutting off rocks, was formed by the erosion and fall of softer veins, the debris being washed away by the sea. The Tintageux and the Autelets shown in this old photograph are masses of detached, angular rocks resembling altars or tables. The Gouliot Caves, on account of their extent and zoological treasures, were reckoned the most famous of Sark caverns. At low water, the visitor could descend by the chimney into the first cavern which cuts through rocks to Havre Gosselin, but a low spring tide was necessary to reach the inner cave with its wealth of anemones. In the 1900s the vicar, the Revd Mr Cachemaille, who took the first party of explorers, described one member, Dr Acland, as 'tearing off specimens with both hands and filling his pockets with sponges.'

The *Liverpool*, wrecked off Alderney, 25 February 1902.

On 25 February 1902 the *Liverpool*, the largest sailing ship wrecked in the Channel Islands, outward bound for San Francisco, became stranded on the north-east end of Alderney near Corblets Bay. One photograph shows attempts being made to salvage cargo while her four masts still carried the great square sails, an astonishing sight. Captain Lewis was judged in error for his handling of the situation.

Islanders from Alderney and Guernsey were drawn as by a magnet, the crew of thirty-seven complaining of theft of their belongings, although a guard was set on the ship and salvaging carried out at the earliest moment. The wreck was bought for £250 and cargo sold off: 1,000 cases and 400 casks of wines and spirits; sardines; olive oil; soap; vinegar; vegetables; 160 bags of sulphur; 3,000 marble slabs; marble table tops; rope; canvas; sails and boats. Efforts to move her failed and months later the sea broke *Liverpool* up. In the late nineteenth century, when she must have refloated, *Liverpool* was reported 'ashore on Sark'.

Courier at Alderney, *c.* 1910.

Another busy vintage photograph of a steamer arrival, this time the *Courier* at Alderney in the early twentieth century. The sail from Guernsey took two hours and in summer season Tuesdays and Thursdays around 9 a.m. and returning 4 p.m. were fixed events, but the boat awaited the arrival of mail from England before departure. Passengers looked out for two finely shaped twin crags at the south-west of the island but most interesting, especially in a gale, was the Swinge, the rock-strewn channel between Alderney and Burhou Island. In 1920 Alderney, with the most bracing climate of all the Channel Islands, had 2,500 inhabitants 'with a decided preponderance of the military element', which perhaps explains the soldiers in the photograph. The one sleepy town, St Anne, situated in the centre of the island, had a few shops and inns, a fine church and a post office. The harbour was built in the mid-nineteenth century, but the construction of a huge breakwater, thought necessary anchorage for the British Fleet – Alderney being strategically an important island, proved to be a costly white elephant never completed.

The Alderney Railway opened in 1847 to transport stone from a quarry to the Admiralty breakwater protecting the harbour. It was in continuous use until the Second World War. *Railway Magazine* reported in 1967 that a lifebuoy was kept in the cab of *Molly II* because on one occasion the train went over the breakwater into the sea. The line was administered by the Ministry of Public Building and Works in the 1960s. It remains the Channel Islands' only working railway. Since 1980 the Alderney Railway Society has operated a service between Braye Road and the Quarry on the old Mineral Railway track.

The Casquets, Alderney.

The Casquets are a group of rocks midway between England and Brittany, 8 miles north-west of Alderney. In shape they resemble a helmet, hence the name, and are notoriously dangerous to shipping. Returning from Normandy, Henry I's son, Prince William, was drowned in the White Ship. The first Casquets Lighthouse on the highest rock was erected in 1790 but since 1726 coal fires were burned on the rocks to signal danger. Swinburne's poem 'Les Casquettes' vividly describes the raging storms and wrecks associated with this area in which the vessels are so vulnerable. Three lighthouses once did duty, St Peter, St Thomas and the Donjon, but in 1872 two were done away with and the remaining improved.

In Longy Bay were found the remains of an ancient forest and it is certain that Alderney was once part of the mainland. Ancient Alderney was known as Monville, an area at the east of the island believed to have been buried by sandstorms. Pottery, spearheads and other Neolithic remains have been found. In medieval days Alderney land was divided into strips.

Near the vicarage of St Anne, the capital of Alderney, farmers used to assemble to decide when vraic should be cut and carted away from beaches at Saline, Crabby, Clonque and Braye, the last mentioned being Alderney's main port in the eighteenth century.

The New Lighthouse, Alderney, 1940.

The New Lighthouse at Alderney was built in 1912, a much-needed beacon, visible for 17 miles. Mannez Lighthouse is a handsome building which can be visited in the afternoon. Fort Les Hommeaux Florains, close to the lighthouse, is ruined and can be reached only by swimming and rock climbing, but on the other side, another of Alderney's forts, Quesnard, can be visited more easily.

During the laying out of a golf course in this area in 1968 an Iron Age site was discovered, possibly a workshop where pots were made as some have been discovered. Four years later a building, possibly Roman, was found across from here at the Kennels. Bronze implements and human remains have been unearthed on Alderney and a megalithic structure, unfortunately destroyed in the nineteenth century, the island's only recorded menhir, La Pierre du Vilain, erected near Longy pond.

The Hanging Rocks, Alderney.

Herm, *c.* 1920.

The islands of Herm and Jethou lie off the east coast of Guernsey. In the 1921 census Herm's population was recorded as '32 and one visitor', Sir Percival Perry being owner at that time. Visitors could view Shell Beach and the Common, but permission to go further had to be applied for at the Herm Estate Office. Shell Beach, extending over half a mile, was then reported as unique in the British Isles, a relic of a long-past epoch when semi-tropical conditions prevailed, for rare shells, not found anywhere else in northern latitudes, were to be seen there. Weather permitting, excursion boats crossed daily from Guernsey during summer. Guernsey, Alderney, Sark, Herm and Jethou together form a Bailiwick quite distinct from Jersey.

The Gate Rock off Herm is pierced by a large hole; supposedly a sixteenth-century mooring place. Belvoir on Herm has a bullock shoeing block. In the nineteenth century, stone quarrying was carried out, which meant a population into the hundreds, but today these quarries are overgrown with furze.

Herm was the home of novelist Compton Mackenzie in the early 1920s and further claim to fame lies in the tiny prison said to be the smallest in the world although that at Jethou must run it a close second.

The Harbour and White House, Herm, 1930.

At the time of this photograph Herm and Jethou could be visited daily by boat from White Rock, Guernsey. At low tide the present-day motor launch stops at La Rosière steps in the Blue Lagoon and at high tide at the harbour pier. This photograph shows the harbour and White House, the latter now one of the most renowned hotels in the Channel Islands, but at the time of this photograph the home of Lord Perry. Still in use on the stone pier of the harbour remains an old crane, a relic of the granite trade. On the slopes of Le Petit Monceau ancient neolithic graves were found, which can still be visited although their contents are housed in Guernsey Museum. The Common on the island, long the home of many rabbits, has a wonderful spring and summer display of wild flowers. Sea birds, notably puffins in their thousands, frequent Plat Houmet, an islet surrounded by masses of rocks. The highest point on the island, 203ft above sea level, is known as the Deer Park. In 1964 the roof of a cave near Pointe Sauzebourge, Le Creux, collapsed after aeons of erosion. Copper mining on Herm was found to be not worthwhile and the attempt abandoned. The cliffs of the private island of Jethou rise to 270ft, compared with Herm's 190ft.

On the coast of Herm, 1930s.

Visitors in the 1930s are taking the coast path on Herm and probably making for the habour in the days when a one penny stamp was all that was required on a postcard. Excavations on Herm in the 1840s revealed the pottery, tools and ornaments of ancient civilisations and indication that the Romans had traded here. No one was living on the island in the seventeenth century, but the nineteenth-century demand for stone led to a population of 400, many of whom were engaged in quarrying material for some of London's most elegant buildings. Belvoir Bay, besides Shell Bay, with its hundreds of species, also has a beautiful beach and unusual shells. Visitors could reach it from the harbour, passing the 200-year-old manor house and the chapel of St Tugal whose original site was the short piece of land which once joined Herm to Jethou. It is said that a storm in the seventh century separated the two islands. Herm at one time formed a parish with Sark.

ACKNOWLEDGEMENTS

I should like to thank all those people who helped in the compiling of this book, not only for their willingness to give information but for their impressive speed and efficiency in sending it. Full marks to fellow-librarians in the Channel Islands!

J. Kenneth Antill; Blackpool Stamp Shop; the late Kate Briggs; Mick Brown, Gorey; British Channel Island Ferries; G.A. Burgess; Department of Tourism and Recreation; Miss C. Easterbrook; Flying Flowers; Friquet Butterfly Farm; The Guernsey Maritime Trust; The Guernsey Press; Guernsey Telephone Museum; Horace Halewood; the late Edward William Houghton; *Jersey Evening Post*; Jersey Lavender Ltd; Jersey Museum; Jersey Pottery; Jersey Zoological Park; Des Layton; Fred Mills; National Trust Folk Museum of Guernsey; John Nettles; Premier Pictures, Jersey; Priaulx Library; *Railway Magazine*; Sark Tourism Officer; Ron Severs; States of Guernsey Library Service; States of Guernsey Tourist Information Bureau; States of Jersey Library Services; States Tourist Office; Barbara Strachan; Dr H. Tomlinson; Tom Venables; Tourist Office, Alderney; Harry Williamson.

I especially thank the late Mr Stanley Butterworth, an excellent photographer, who worked wonders to improve the quality of some of these old photographs.

John L. Stoddard.

John L. Stoddard, distinguished lecturer and traveller, photographed in 1874. He travelled the world with his portable dark room, plate camera and black cloth and was commissioned to prepare a popular book portfolio of photographs of famous cities, scenes and paintings containing views of the Pyramids, native tribes and wonders of the world. On a short visit to the Channel Islands he was impressed by the botanical specimens, rocks and shells, some of which he had encountered in faraway lands. For his world trip he sailed on the liner RMS *Oceanic*, one of the fleet known as the White Star Line founded by T.H. Ismay in 1869. Stoddard reported: 'Jersey is a populous island covering 40,000 acres, an island of fruit and flowers full of beauty both of land and sea with a climate, impossible to surpass'. He was impressed with Mont Orgueil Castle, 'built upon the solid rock and some bits of it are said to be Roman but most of the building belongs to the twelfth century.'